VIKKI L. PENDLETON

BECOMING A WEALTHY BELIEVER Part 2

The Believer's Keys To Success

Contents

Introduction

Dear Chosen,

Hopefully this will be a short and to the point introduction of my first book. It's been a long time coming because I had to learn so much that took years of many experiences to grow into.

My government name is Vikki LeTonya Pendleton. My nickname is Sugar. I am a Christian Hip Hop artist and Christian stage DJ for concerts and Christian events that have performers. Please listen to my music on any listening format. You can find it under my artist's name DJ JChill or DJ JCHILL. (Some formats are case sensitive).

JCHILL is an acronym for Jesus Christ Has Infinite Lasting Love.

Once this book hits the market, I will be offering services for Power Couple Contracts, Matrimony Contracts, Consultation help finding your Divine Purpose, Consultation on developing into becoming a Chosen vessel, specifically tailored daily affirmations for you, Speaking engagements, conferences, conventions, book signings, music performances, concerts, and Stage DJ formats.

All characters in this book are fictional characters for the purpose of illustrating my point or example.

The purpose of this book is to explain to God's Chosen vessels how to create and maintain a successful and wealthy lifestyle by using key strategies in the Bible for walking in your Divine purpose. Often times throughout the book I will make reference to a "key" which is noting an important point for wealth building.

Certain things are repeated consistently throughout the Bible. In my book I also repeat certain things consistently. The purpose of this repetition within the Bible is the same purpose for the repetition in this book, it is because it is of strong importance and most people ignore this particular important thing. The more you hear it, the more apt you will be to grasp it. Therefore, I repeat it and I give repeated different scenarios hoping that the Chosen vessel will understand the importance and adopt the certain characteristic that I am repeating because it is a must that it be mastered by the Chosen.

Becoming a Wealthy Believer is a trilogy. Please read the first book if you have not done so already and then move on to the third.

Thank you to all who believed in me, you know who you are. And thank you to all that didn't, you know who you are too. I am Vikki the Victorious Victor, I guess you didn't know the meaning of my name.

With All My Love,
   Vikki aka Sugar aka JCHILL

1

CHAPTER 1

PSALMS BOOK 1

Happy are those who don't listen to the wicked,
　　Who don't go where sinners go,
　　Who doesn't do what evil people do.
　　They love the Lord's teachings day and night.
　　They are strong, like a tree planted by a river.
　　The tree produces fruit in its season,
　　And its leaves don't die.
　　Everything they do will succeed.
　　But wicked people are not like that.
　　They are like chaff that the wind blows away.
　　So, the wicked will not escape God's punishment,
　　Sinners will not worship with God's people.
　　This is because the Lord takes care of his people,
　　But the wicked will be destroyed.

The book of Psalms 1 is my favorite passage in the Bible. It is one of the main keys to prosperity. It is packed with wisdom that is magical.

I reiterate, happiness is a choice. If you choose to do as this passage tells you, you will be happy and free of depression and anxiety. You can't get advice or counsel from ungodly people, you can't do what the ungodly people do, you can't even go to the ungodly places that they go to. Instead, you must read, study, and meditate on God's Word, day, and night.

By doing so, God will take care of you. The result is: every endeavor you embark upon will be successful in your season.

2

CHAPTER 2

ALL THINGS WORK TOGETHER

It is an illusion to think that you can live in this world without any type of hardship or any type of problems. Just because you are reading and studying the word of God and implementing what it says daily, does not mean problems will not arise in your life. The Bible clearly says that trials and tribulations come but to make you strong. You must go through hardships and problems to grow spiritually and mentally. It's how you gain wisdom and knowledge aside from the knowledge that you acquired through your reading and studying. The trials and errors of life will make you stronger. Your experiences as you go through life will grow you and give you wisdom.

The key to learning and growing through your hardships, problems, and trials, is in how you respond to them. You need to have the understanding that there is nothing that you can't get through in this life if you have your faith, and you know that God is on your side. When you are sure without a doubt, that God has already worked a solution in your favor, your response will always be one of calmness filled with faith. You know from Psalms 1 that if you are not seeking the counsel of the ungodly or doing things that the ungodly do, and you are reading the word of God and studying the word of

God, that God will take care of you. Part of taking care of you includes getting you through tough situations in a favorable way.

And you know that all things work together for the good to those who love God, to those who are called according to his purpose. Romans 8:28. When you read this passage, you must know that it is talking about those who love God. Those who love God show that they love God by obeying His word, by studying His word, and by spreading His word.

A person that loves God will not intentionally do harm or wrong to cause problems or hardships and then expect God to make it right. Romans 8:28 is describing a person going through life's daily ups and downs because of his love for Christ and him doing the will of God by doing what he was created and called by God to do. Your mission alone will cause problems for you as we go through life.

You are created with a purpose, and you will fulfill that purpose in the correct season for that purpose to manifest. If that season has not yet come for you, God will still make sure all things work out for your good so that you are ready when your season comes for you to operate in that calling. It is very safe to say that many of the trials and tribulations you encounter before you embark upon your calling, is preparation for when it is your season to birth that which God has placed within you to do. Each talent that you have has its own season, some overlapping.

You are an earthly target for the enemy to try to stop you from fulfilling the destiny you were created to do. Rest assured; God got your back.

No matter how enticing it is to do what the ungodly does, stay away from it, it's a set up for failure!

3

CHAPTER 3

THE LEADER YOU ARE

Let's use the Biblical story of Joseph as an example of serving others as the leader you are. The name "Joseph" means "may God increase". We can see from the name alone that God is going to give Joseph great increase regardless of how his beginning may look. Names are important. They have significance in who you are and who you will become.

Jacob, Joseph's father, was a twin. Jacob's mother favored Jacob, and his father favored his twin Esau. This favoritism caused a lot of grief in the family and between the twin brothers. Jacob had 12 children of his own, and he favored his 11th son, Joseph. Here we see Jacob did not learn from the lesson he went through as a child. He knows from firsthand experience that showing favoritism between children in the same family can cause great hardship and can even destroy families. Yet he did not learn from that experience, and he carried on the generational curse and showed favoritism amongst his own children to one child.

1. Learn from your own personal lessons when leading others. Do not repeat bad habits or bad actions that you experienced firsthand when

you are in your own role of leadership.

Jacob had a long, expensive robe made for Joseph. He didn't have such a robe made for any of the other children and it was obvious he did this for Joseph because that was the child he favored. He didn't care about the feelings of the other children when he made this gesture and it angered Josephs brothers and made them jealous causing them to hate Joseph.

1. Do not show favoritism amongst those you lead or raise as your children. You can reward when rewards are due, but don't just outwardly praise and give gifts for no apparent reason other than you really like the individual. This will cause the others you lead to harbor feelings of jealousy and anger towards that person and even you.

Joseph started having dreams. In the dreams he was shown that he would one day be in a leadership position over his family. Joseph shared these dreams with his siblings and his parents. In the first dream each of the brothers had a bundle of wheat, and Joseph's bundle was standing up above them all, and his brother's bundles were bowed down. Second dream, Joseph saw the sun, the moon, and 11 stars. Which represented his father, his mother, and his eleven brothers. He saw all of them bow down to him. The sun bowed to him, the moon bowed to him, and all eleven stars bowed down to Joseph. When Joseph shared these dreams with his family his father was disturbed by the dreams, and his older brothers were angry and very upset.

1. It is not wise to tell others how you will rule over them in a powerful position. Even if you know you will be elevated to a higher position, do not boast about it, it will cause others to despise you. Once you are in that position of leadership, stay humble. You can't lead those who don't like you. Be a likable person.

One day Joseph's father sent him to the hills where his older brothers were. When his older brothers saw Joseph coming, they decided to kill Joseph, and throw his body into a pit, and then they were going to lie to their father and say that a wild animal attacked Joseph and killed him. And one of the brothers said, "then we shall see what becomes of his dreams!"

1. Do not plan or plot wrongdoings against other people. Always be honest, and do not lie.

This plan bothered the oldest brother, Reuben. And he had to think quickly to suggest something other than doing this to Joseph. He suggested that they throw Joseph into a pit and then leave him in the pit for dead. And Reuben had planned to secretly go and rescue Joseph later when the brothers weren't around. The brothers accepted this proposal and thought it was a good idea to do. When Joseph got close enough to them, they seized him and they ripped off his beautiful coat that his father gave to him, and they threw him down into a pit. Several other brothers remained near the pit, and they sat down to eat. They saw some traders on their way to Egypt pass by and they came up with the idea of selling Joseph to them and getting money for Joseph instead of letting him die in the pit. Ruben was gone and so Joseph didn't have anyone to advocate for him and his older brothers sold him at 17 years old into slavery for 20 pieces of silver.

1. Always advocate for others, and treat them fairly, even if it's something about them that you don't like.

A little bit later in the evening, Reuben went to the pit in secret where Joseph was supposed to be, and he saw that Joseph was missing. Reuben then went to his brothers very upset telling them that the boy was gone and what is it that he should do now? The brothers told him that they were going to dip Joseph coat in goat's blood and pretend that a wild beast had killed Joseph and show the coat as proof to their father that Joseph was killed by the beast. Reuben went along with his brother's story, and they showed their father the coat with the blood on it saying Joseph was dead. When Jacob saw the blood on Joseph's coat, he cried so hard, and no one could comfort him.

1. Do not intentionally bring grief and hardship to other people. Instead, always be a person of compassion and comfort.
2. Do not go along with other people's false stories to keep from looking like the oddball or from being ridiculed for standing on the truth. Always stand on truth.

Joseph was sold to a man named Potiphar; he was the captain of pharaoh's guards. Overtime Potiphar recognized Joseph skill and his trustworthiness, and he made Joseph a steward over his estate. But Potiphar's wife thought that Joseph was very handsome, and she was always trying to seduce Joseph. One time she grabbed him by his garment, and he pulled away from her. She then was very hurt because he continued to reject her, so she accused him of attempting to rape her and used his garment as evidence. Joseph was once again thrown back into prison.

1. If you are experiencing sexual harassment of any kind, it is best to bring it forward to those above your position because if you keep quiet about it the situation will only escalate and get worse.
2. Do not harass or sexually harass anyone in any way.

Joseph was in prison with Pharaoh's personal cup bearer and Pharaoh's personal Baker. Both men had peculiar dreams, and when they told Joseph that no interpretation was possible, Joseph explained to them that true interpretations come from God, and he offered to go to God of Israel on their behalf and get the meaning of their dreams. The men began to tell Joseph their dreams. Joseph then prayed to God to get the meaning of the dreams. Joseph told the cup bearer that Pharaoh was going to free him in three days, and he told the Baker that Pharaoh would execute him in three days. Everything that Joseph said came true in three days. The cup bearer returned to his duties in the court and forgot all about Joseph. And the Baker was executed just as Joseph said.

1. Always use your God given talents and gifts while serving others as a

leader. Don't be afraid to share the goodness of God with those who are around you and always pray for them.

About two years later, Pharaoh had a dream that he was standing by the Nile River and 7 skinny cows, and seven fat cows came out of the water. The skinny famished cows ate up the fat cows. And this was followed by 7 wilted ears of grain eating up 7 healthy ears of grain. The dream disturbed Pharaoh so bad he couldn't rest, and he sent from magicians and wise men to ask for an interpretation. No one was able to interpret Pharaoh's dream. The cup bearer remembered that Joseph interpreted his dream when he was in prison, and he told Pharaoh about that incident, and how the interpretation came true as Joseph said. He told Pharoah how markable Joseph was and Pharaoh sent for Joseph right away.

1. 1 Corinthians 15:58 says, "therefore my beloved brethren, be ye steadfast, unmovable, always abounding in the work of the Lord, for as much as you know that your labor is not in vain in the Lord." Galatians 6:9 says, "Do not be weary in well doing: for in due season, you will reap if you faint not." Your day of promotion is coming, your great works are being recognized and you will be rewarded! So just hang in there. Do not be weary in well doing and don't quit.

When Joseph heard Pharaoh's dream, he knew it was a warning and he sent the interpretation of the warning to Pharaoh. This is the interpretation he gave, "God has revealed to Pharaoh what He is about to do, there will be seven good years which will be followed by seven years of terrible famine". Then, Joseph outlined a plan so that the Egyptians could be saved from starvation. This plan pleased Pharaoh so much that he made Joseph an overseer of the Kingdom and gave him the authority to organize grain storage for the next seven years.

1. Always have a plan. Never try to just wing it when you are in a leadership position. That's not what leaders do, leaders write down their plan and

implement what they have written.

2. Always heed the warning signs; never dismiss a warning.
3. If you see disaster coming, look out for those under your leadership and devise a plan to keep them safe.

Within these first 7 years, Joseph met and married and Egyptian woman, and they had two sons together. When the famine came, all the other nations starved, but the Egyptians kept bread on every table because of Joseph's wonderful planning. The famine was so bad that even in Canaan, Jacob and his sons had absolutely no food to eat. So, Jacob sent Joseph's 10 older brothers to Egypt to buy grain, and he kept Benjamin, who was the youngest and 12th child, with him. When the brothers were brought before Joseph, Joseph immediately recognized them, but they did not recognize who Joseph was.

1. Always protect the children. Do not allow them to be in harm's way.
2. Pay attention to who is in your circle, recognize them for who they are.

Immediately Joseph accused his brothers of spying and he had them sent to prison. His brothers begged to be released because they were innocent and said that they were not spies by are 10 of 11 sons of the same man and they only wanted food. Joseph still did not reveal himself and he sold them grain but made them promise to return with their younger brother, and he kept his brother named Simeon behind as hostage to ensure that they would return. Joseph then hid their payment for the grain in their bags, giving them their money back secretly. On their journey home the nine brothers discovered the money, and they got scared that if they went back to Egypt they would be accused of stealing. When they told Jacob their father what had happened Jacob said he would let Benjamin return with them only if Reuben offered the lives of his own two sons and Judah offered to take the blame if anything happens. The brothers then went back to Egypt, and to their great relief, Joseph welcomed them into his home. At the site of Benjamin Joseph had to leave the room because he had started crying.

1. Revenge belongs to God on our behalf. Do not be revengeful or hold grudges.
2. Do not take from the poor, instead give to the needy.
3. What good deeds you do for others in secret, God will reward you openly.
4. Do not allow fear to cause you to miss out on your blessings. Fear is not a Godly characteristic.

Joseph's brothers purchased more grain from Joseph. However, Joseph wanted to keep Benjamin with him, so he hid a silver cup in Benjamin's backpack with the money his brothers gave him to purchase the grain. When Joseph's servants found the cup and the money in Benjamin's backpack, they had Benjamin arrested. Judah begged on his knees before Joseph for the life of his youngest brother Benjamin. When Joseph heard that their father Jacob might die of a broken heart and sorrow if Benjamin didn't come back with them, he sent his servants out of the room, and he told his brothers who he really was. His brothers were shocked when Joseph expressed no desire for further revenge but instead, he cried so loud that almost everybody in Egypt heard him. Joseph said to his brothers, "it was not you who sent me here, but it was God".

1. Don't plant false evidence on anyone. Don't try to purposely get someone in trouble.
2. God will prepare a table for you in front of your enemies. You will always rise above those who do you wrong. "Do not touch my anointed ones and do my prophets no harm". This is mentioned twice in the Bible so it's serious business to God. 1 Chronicles 16:22 and Psalm 105:15.
3. God will always turn what was meant for your harm or bad, to good and in your favor. Hold on to that while you serve others as a leader.

When pharaoh found out that Josephs brothers had come and purchased grain, he sent his wagons to bring Joseph's family back to Egypt. Josephs 11 brothers went to Canaan taking loads of gifts to their father from Joseph. Joseph gave Benjamin extra. When Joseph's brothers told Jacob that Joseph was alive and governor in Egypt, Jacob didn't believe it. Jacob saw all the wonderful gifts and livestock Joseph sent to him and he began to believe. Then God spoke to Jacob and told him not to be afraid to go to Egypt because Joseph is there, and he will indeed see him, and God assured Jacob that He will be with him as he goes to Egypt. Then they all return to Egypt with Jacob, a total of 70 people in the caravans that Pharaoh sent for them. Jacob was now elderly at 130 years old, but he was overjoyed to get to Egypt at the promise of seeing his favorite son Joseph that he thought was dead. Joseph never returned to Canaan alive except for one time and that was to bury his father. Pharaoh gave Jacob's sons and their families land in Goshen away from the Egyptians who were prejudice against sheepherders.

The faithfulness of Joseph, even when he was wrongly imprisoned, not once but twice, spilled over to be a blessing to his entire family. Joseph also demonstrated what true forgiveness looks like.

We see the compassion of Joseph when he realizes that in his absence, his father favored his younger brother Benjamin as he once did Joseph. He felt Benjamin's pain because he knew that meant the older brothers were jealous of Benjamin and treated him unfairly as they once did him. Having been in that same lonely and heartbreaking place as the favored younger brother, Joseph cried with compassion for Benjamin. He knew his pain, so much so that he wanted to keep Benjamin with him to free him of the painful position he was born into.

1. Racial and economic prejudice is real and still prevalent today. But do not allow that to stop you from doing what God has called you to do. You are not alone; God is with you every step of the way.
2. To be a proficient and effective leader, you must be a forgiving person. People will be people, and people are not perfect. People will do things to you that will call for your forgiveness. Be very forgiving. It works in your favor.
3. Be aware of the pain and suffering of each person you serve as a leader.

Joseph was destined for greatness from the time he was formed in the womb of his mother. God showed Joseph in dreams as a young boy that he would grow up and have a position of power, and even rule over his family in that position. Young Joseph may not have understood what the dreams meant in its entirety, but he knew they were from God, and he knew he was going to grow up to be more than a sheep herdsman. Even the prejudice of the Egyptians against his kind did not stop him from having a position of power over even them.

When God has placed a calling on your life and shows you that you are destined for greatness, it is the job of the enemy to try to stop your flow. But if you continue in your faithfulness nothing can stop what God has destined for your life. All those who wronged you, who didn't believe in you, who scandalized your name, and wanted you dead, will witness your strength, your steadfastness, your obedience to God, and your will to accomplish that which God created you to do.

1. Pray to God about everything and seek His will on how to handle situations and how to plan concerning the people you serve.
2. Be aware that you look and behave differently when you are in a leadership position. Joseph recognized his brothers because they were in the same position that he last saw them in, but Joseph was unrecognizable to them because his new position caused him to look and behave differently than when they last saw him. Higher positions come from growth. You don't look the same when you elevate.

4

CHAPTER 4

NOT PROCRASTINATING

Procrastination is a sin. Laziness regarding your work is a brother to the master of destruction. Just like our talents are a gift from God, so is time. The fact that we are still here and have time to so what we were created to do is a gift from God. Procrastination is the act of willfully putting off doing something that should be done. That is wasting time and wasting our talents. It's a sin.

There are different reasons why people procrastinate. Fear is a big reason. Overscheduling is another. When I'm upset or angry, I put things off and procrastinate because I can't concentrate on what I should be doing. How we are feeling emotionally is a huge factor in procrastinating for a lot of people.

Procrastinating will cause you to miss out on blessings. You are Divinely rewarded for doing what God has instructed you to do. You will walk in His favor when you are obedient to God's will. If you are procrastinating, then you aren't walking in God's favor, nor are you being rewarded for doing the will of God for your life.

As soon as opposition comes, people want God to get them out of the situation, but they were procrastinating on doing what God has created them to do. That's a bit lopsided in my opinion. What if God procrastinated when people need Him? Thank goodness He doesn't treat people the way they treat Him.

Bottom line is, you will accomplish nothing when you procrastinate. Stop being lazy and create. You will be rewarded greatly for doing so.

5

CHAPTER 5

THE TITHES

I always say we must tithe our Time, Talents, and Treasure. To tithe is a major key component to wealth building. It's so simple, it's the law of giving and receiving. You must give to receive. You don't give, you don't receive. The more you give, the more you receive.

If you are procrastinating, then you are not tithing your time. If you are not volunteering to help others in some compacity, then you aren't tithing your time. If you aren't planning out your Divine goals and dreams, then you aren't tithing your time. If you aren't reading and studying God's Word, then you aren't tithing your time. If you aren't praying constantly to God, then you are not tithing your time, because you aren't giving your time to God or to edify God. And God is the One who has given you Time in the first place. You have 24 hours in a day, 2 hours, and 24 minutes at the very least should be tithed to God.

You must tithe your talents as well. That means using your talent without pay for the edification of Christ. Without pay is the key word. If you are getting paid to play the organ then you are not tithing, you are doing a paid job. Your talents and gifts are to be used to build up others and tithing them means you are freely giving your talents and gifts to help others. If you have a business, you can give free hours or free products that you have created as a tithe. People have so many different talents, whatever yours is, tithe a portion of it.

Finally, tithe at least ten percent of your earned income. Off the top, give ten percent and then budget with the rest. I iterate budget because that's the smart thing to do with your money. You need to be a good steward of the treasure God gives to you. When you don't budget, you may spend frivolously.

Tithers are so super blessed. I can't even explain how blessed you are when you tithe. Blessings drop out of the sky it seems. Other people will look at you and wonder how you do it...but it's God blessing you for being a faithful tither of your Time, Talents, and Treasure. The Bible tells you if you tithe like you should the Lord will open the floodgates of Heaven and pour out so many blessing that you will not have room enough to receive it! Try me in this, says the Lord.

Jesus said, "If you give, you will receive. Your gift will return to you in full measure, pressed down, shaken together to make room for more, and running over. Whatever measure you use in giving — -large or small — -it will be used to measure what is given back to you." Luke 6:38.

With that being said, I have some advice for you. Make sure you are tithing on fertile ground. Meaning, do not tithe to evil doers or those who aren't appreciative. Tithing is planting a seed and if seeds aren't planted on fertile ground they will not grow and produce fruit. You want your seed to grow and produce fruit because that is the part that we eat for nourishment. In other words, **to get a return** on what you have given, it needs to be towards a good cause. Otherwise, it is just a waste of your tithe.

6

CHAPTER 6

THE POWER OF FAITH

You must read Hebrews Chapter 11; the power of faith is so astonishing! This chapter tells you so many stories of people in the Bible who used their faith and did miraculous things. Chapter 11 starts off by telling us exactly what faith is. It says, "now faith is the substance of things hoped for, the evidence of things not seen. By faith we understand that the worlds were framed by the word of God so that the things which are seen were not made of things which are visible". That is so deep! That is verse 1 and verse 3, verse 6 says, "but without faith it is impossible to please God for he who comes to God must believe that He is and that He is a rewarder of those who diligently seek him".

I have come to tell you that just by using faith you can do incredible miracles. The wealth in having great faith is immeasurable. When you have the assured confidence that whatever you hope for is going to happen, you are working miracles that others cannot understand. It's a miracle because it is surely going to manifest. They don't understand because they don't have that level of faith.

Assuming that you already believe that God is, the first thing you need to do to achieve this level of faith, is get rid of all negative thinking. You can't have faith and be pessimistic at the same time. Having faith is an act of optimism. You can't have doubt, or think maybe it will, you must know that without a doubt what it is you are believing God for will manifest into the natural.

The second thing you need to do is change your way of thinking. Think on all things that are good and positive. Do not entertain ungodly thoughts at all. Keep your mind pure with clear, clean, thoughts. Digest God's word daily because it increases the level of your faith as well as keeps your mind on things from above. No dark gutter thoughts.

The third thing you need to do is surround yourself with Godly people who are full of faith. You can't have ungodly people as your crowd of choice, and you try to manifest miracles through faith. They will mock you and make fun of you which will destroy your confidence and tear down your spirit man.

Now you can activate your faith and bring forth what you are hoping for. If you are sick, claim your healing and thank God for it. Believe it and you will be healed. Even diseases that man says is incurable, will leave your body and you will be free of it. If you want a promotion within your job with higher pay, pray about it, work towards it, believe it is coming, and watch it happen!

Make sure that what you are believing in is within the will of God. With little to no faith, we hold up our blessings from the Lord. With great faith we are merely opening the door for what God already has for us. So many people never tap into the plans of prosperity that God has for them because they have so little faith.

"For I know the plans I have for you", declares the Lord, "plans to prosper you and not to harm you, plans to give you hope and a future." Jeremiah 29:11. Believe this without a doubt and take your God given talent and use it knowing that it will prosper you through the Grace of God!

7

CHAPTER 7

BE THANKFUL FOR THE SMALL THINGS

The way to be ruler of much is to be thankful for the little you have. The more gratitude you have, the more increase you will gain. You must be sincerely thankful and grateful for what God has blessed you with.

You cannot be constantly wanting what somebody else has, wishing you had more than you have, and complaining about what you do have. There is always someone who has less than you. And there's always someone who has more than you. But your main concern should just be you and being thankful that you are still here on earth living and breathing and able to increase all that you have already.

The prayer of Jabez is such a powerful passage that whole books have been written about it. Songs have been sung about the whole prayer of Jabez. Out of the entire Bible it is only two verses that mention Jabez! What we know about him is actually very little. But songs and books have been written about his prayer.

1Chronicles 4:9-10 says, Now Jabez was more honorable than his brothers, and his mother called his name Jabez, saying, "Because I bore him in pain." And Jabez called on the God of Israel saying, "Oh, that You would bless me indeed, and enlarge my territory, that Your hand would be with me, and that You would keep me from evil, that I may not cause pain!" So, God granted him what he requested.

That is what the entire Bible says about Jabez. That's it.

Jabez was aware of his name. His name meant he brings pain. He didn't want to cause pain to anyone else anymore, which obviously brought pain to him that he somehow, because we don't know how other than in childbirth, he brought pain to other people. If he wasn't still bringing pain to people, he would not have included it in his prayer. The pain included something that was evil according to his prayer, and he didn't want that anymore.

We see that he was close to God, and closer than his siblings because it says he was more honorable than his brothers. He believed in the power of prayer, and he prayed in faith because God granted him what he requested. It is only our faith when we pray that activates the movement of God. Praying in doubt doesn't even hit the ceiling.

Jabez asked God to increase his territory. He asked to be given more than what he already has. Being that he was honorable towards God, we know Jabez was very grateful for what he already had, but he wanted an increase. And because of his gratefulness, sincereness, and being a more honorable man than those around him, God increased his territory.

Being sincerely grateful and thankful for what you have been blessed with and recognizing what you do have as blessings from God, and not what you acquired on your own accord, will get you increase when you pray it.

8

CHAPTER 8

WHAT YOU SOW IS WHAT YOU REAP

Whether you are a believer or non-believer certain laws apply and reaping what you sow is one of those laws. It's the boomerang effect, what you do, what you think, and what you say will return to you at some point in your life. I have mentioned it several times in this book because it can't be said enough. It's one of those things we know, but we forget, when we should be remembering. Too many times we do, say, and think things hastily without first weighing the consequence or the return of the boomerang we just released.

I mentioned in a prior section of this book how important it is to give of yourself to others, using time, talents, and/or treasures, and it will come back to you, and it usually comes back with an increase. If you sow bad seed, meaning if you are gossiping, stealing, lying, cheating, etc., that is the heartache you will get back in return, and usually in an increased magnitude. Most of the time when people are talking about sowing and reaping, they are talking about your actions, or what you say, coming back to you. I rarely hear anyone mention sowing and reaping when it is pertaining to what you think. I want to take this portion of the book and enlighten you on the "what you think" aspect of reaping and sowing.

"What a man thinks in his heart, such is he." What we think and how we think is who we are. How we move and govern ourselves is a direct reflection of how we think. We can choose to be happy, or we can cause suffering upon ourselves just by how we think and what we think about.

For example, in intimate relationships, one partner can be thinking that their partner is cheating when the other partner is late coming home and not answering the cellphone. As a result, they began to think all kinds of negative emotions which brings emotional suffering upon their self unnecessarily by their mind going rapid with ideas of how their partner is cheating on them. When the partner gets home it is revealed that they were stuck in traffic and had no way to call because the cell phone was dead. More than likely, the way the first partner was thinking shows the insecurities from their past experiences with a cheating mate, and now this person moves as an insecure individual within intimate relationships by merely the way they think, which causes a hardship on the relationship. They may go from relationship to relationship because the insecure thoughts that they sow, comes out as negative actions on their part. In return they reap failed relationships. All from a wrong and bad thought.

How and what you think has a direct effect on what materializes in your life. If you sow good thoughts, you reap good fruit. If you sow bad thoughts, you reap bad fruit. And this is so because what you think is who you are. Just by the way you think you can control and determine your life experiences and choose what materializes in your life. Because how you think is how you will move.

If little Johnny thinks the best way to help his family eat and survive is to steal, then little Johnny will become a thief and eventually end up in prison. But if Little Johnny thinks the best way to help his family eat and survive is to go to school and master the game of basketball so he will have scholarships for a college education, Little Johnny will end up with a college degree and just might go to the NBA to support his family and help them out of poverty. Or at least an education for him to not repeat the cycle of poverty. How Little Johnny thinks will determine what he will reap. Because his actions will reflect his thoughts. Your thoughts direct your actions.

Another way we sow seeds is through our thought process. Many of our thoughts take root and grow, or they do the opposite, and the thought goes nowhere and doesn't produce anything. Let's look at Lisa who is an opera singer. She currently only sings at her church. She has the thought of singing on Broadway in musicals. This thought takes root and grows as she ponders ideas on how to become an opera singer on Broadway. A couple months later she googles and finds a local opera ensemble and reaches out to a member through social media. That member invites her to audition at the next practice and Lisa blew them out the water and landed a seat in the local opera ensemble. A year later Lisa's local ensemble traveled to Broadway to watch a musical play. Lisa takes the opportunity to reach out to a cast member afterwards and landed an audition for that musical and got it! She packed her stuff and moved right away to pursue her dream that started with a thought. Lisa became the highest paid Opera singer in history! Okay I made that up, but you get the picture.

What if Lisa dismissed the thought by telling herself, after having the thought, that she wasn't good enough for Broadway? Lisa would not have accomplished that dream and become the highest paid opera singer in history. That would be someone else's story that had the same thought and pursued it.

Manifestation starts with your thoughts. You can manifest good, or you can manifest bad. It all depends on how you think. What you manifest is what you are reaping.

Have you ever heard of people who believe their own lies? This is a true process because they tell the lie to themselves and maybe even to others, and the lie takes root and grows inside of them. As they continue to think about the lie, they will begin to believe the lie. This happens because the lie has taken root and is growing in their mind. The lie begins to manifest inside of them and eventually spilling outwardly, and this person will begin to act outwardly in a way as if the lie is true. What they are reaping, and manifesting is bad fruit because it developed from a lie. The effect this outward action will have on their life will not be one that is good. This person sowed a bad seed of thought and in return they will reap bad fruit.

The thoughts that you think in your mind is going to determine what you say, how you move, and ultimately, what you reap. This is why Paul said in the Bible, "Finally, brethren, whatsoever things are true, whatsoever things are honest, whatsoever things are just, whatsoever things are pure, whatsoever things are lovely, whatsoever things are of good report; if there be any virtue, and if there be any praise, **think on these things**". This is how you harvest, reap, and manifest good fruit.

You create and manifest your environment by the way you think. If you work 15 to 17 hours a day on a job that you don't even like to get your paycheck, and that's all you expect, then that's all you will get. If you think about your talent and how you can use it to create wealth and act on your thoughts and seek out the avenue you need to take to manifest wealth from using your talent, that's exactly what you will create. Just from your thought process. If you can think it, you can do it.

Here is the kicker: Inside of each Believer is the Holy Spirit. But also, each Believer has his fleshy desires. Each person has a good voice and a bad voice inside of them and it's up to that person to decide which voice he chooses to listen to. You must bring every thought into captivity and decide where the thought came from and if it is to be thrown out or planted in your mind.

With the Holy Spirit inside of you, you now have the power of the Almighty God to implement every good thought. You have inside of you, working for and through you, everything that you need to create the life for yourself that you envision. The God that lives in you will reveal to you everything you need to know to accomplish this dream, because He is the One who placed the dream in your mind from the beginning with the thought of an idea.

Every attribute that God is, dwells inside of you and you can access that power to create wealth and manifest the life you envision for yourself freely because it is the will of God for your life already. The seven gifts of the Holy Spirit are wisdom, understanding, counsel, fortitude, knowledge, piety, and fear of the Lord. Fortitude is defined as courage in pain or adversity. You are equipped with everything you need within you to create wealth.

In keeping your thoughts pure, be sure not to covet or envy what someone else has. This is sowing a negative seed, and you will reap negative results in your own life. We are to rejoice with our brothers and sisters and not harbor jealous thoughts towards them. By rejoicing with them and being genuinely happy for them, and by thinking good and positive thoughts concerning their victory, you are sowing good seeds and will reap good seeds in your own life in due season. When you think negative thoughts of envy and jealousy, it is the boomerang you threw out and it's coming back to you. Wealth will avoid you because you do not rejoice in it with others.

Watch this: What if you not only rejoice with others when they receive blessings, but you truly want even more for them! Imagine what the boomerang will bring back to YOU! The abundance is YOUR CUP RUNNING OVER SO MUCH SO THAT YOU WON'T HAVE ROOM TO RECEIVE IT ALL!!!!!!

The reason you don't have enough room to receive it all is because you are to give to others and God makes sure we have enough overflow to give and be a blessing to others. And the cycle continues, as you continue to give, you continue to receive. You can't change the law of sowing and reaping, but you can definitely use it to your advantage, with a pure heart, and it's all according to the way you think.

9

CHAPTER 9

TIME AND GOD'S TIMING

Memory is the ongoing process of information retention over time. We remember past events and hold on to them because we can't go back in time and relive them. The only thing we can do about the past is remember it. It's time that we can't get back ever again. It's history.

Time is the continued sequence of existence and events that occur in an apparently irreversible succession from the past, through the present, into the future. Our entire state of being exists and evolves around time.

There is great value in time, and how you use your time determines your level of wealth building during your time living on Earth. But even greater than that, is God's timing.

If we need to be somewhere at a certain time, we can get there early, late, or on time. With God's timing it is only one way, and that is on time. God doesn't show up late or early, He is an On Time God. Therefore, we need to be careful not to confuse our existence in time with God's timing for our life events. Every blessing, every occasion, every trial, every event, that caused for God to show up in your life, He showed up on time. And let me add, it doesn't matter at what age you actually walk in your calling, it is right on time. God chooses when it is our season, not us. There are specific people that need what God has placed in us to give, and when that season arises, and we deliver, it's on time. God's time.

Please enjoy my humor in this illustration:

Remember when Jesus went to Mary and Martha house and Martha was so busy cleaning and cooking for Jesus and Mary was sitting at Jesus feet listening to Him talk, and Martha got so angry? Then another time Jesus went to their house and Mary poured her expensive perfume on Jesus' feet and wiped them with her hair? Well Mary, Martha, and Lazarus were siblings, and they all lived together in Bethany. The Bible says Jesus loved them, and we see that Jesus was a frequent visitor, so we know that they were dear friends. (We don't go to people's houses that we don't like).

One day Lazarus became very sick, and his sisters sent a message to Jesus and said, "Lord the one you love is sick." When Jesus got the message he said, "Lazarus's sickness will not end in death. No, it is for the glory of God. I, the Son of God, will receive glory from this." Jesus stayed right where he was for the next two days and did not go to them.

Jesus had just left from them when Martha was mad at Mary for not helping her cook and clean and when he got ready to finally go to see what was up concerning Lazarus, He said to His disciples, "Let's go to Judea **again**."

Mary and Martha did not hear Jesus say that this was going to be a miracle that would give God glory and Lazarus will not end in death. Jesus said that to His disciples and Jesus did not send a message back to Mary and Martha so they would know. Now the Bible makes mention, that although Jesus loved Mary, Martha, and Lazarus, he stayed where he was for two more days. (Just because God does not show up when YOU want Him to, does not mean that He does not love you. It means, it's not time yet).

Just imagine needing your best friend who you love, and they love you, and your friend doesn't show up for you. You send word for them to come, and they dismiss what you say, don't even return your call, and then come when it's too late! You may not even be their friend anymore after that. Especially Martha because we see she is already hot tempered. So, Mary and Martha were probably in Bethany upset with Jesus.

Then on top of Jesus not coming right away, His disciples didn't want Him to go! They tried to stop Him from going saying he was almost killed in Judea two days ago. Why in the world was He really going back there again?

You know Jesus, He used that opportunity to hint around at the certain disciples that be in the streets partying at night but supposed to be followers of Christ. He said, "Look, there are twelve hours of daylight every day. As long as it is light, people can walk safely. They can see because they have the light of this world. Only at night is there danger of stumbling because there is no light." He paused so it could sink in, then He said, "Our friend Lazarus has fallen asleep, but now I will go and wake him up."

Jesus was saying It's twelve hours in the day, do what you going to do during the daytime, because the freaks come out at night, it's not safe in these streets at night. And God's people don't need to be out there stumbling around at night in this dark world. (I'm just kidding, that's not what Jesus meant, but it is truth to it).

This is what Jesus meant: The Day represented walking in the will of God and being protected because you are in God's will. The Night represented doing things in the absence of God's will. That will cause you to stumble for sure. Jesus was saying He is doing the will of God and He will be protected.

The disciples were kind of slow in this moment because they were like, "listen, Jesus, if Lazarus is sleeping that means he is getting better!" Jesus gets irritated with the disciples because they are acting like they are mentally slow, so He plainly says, "Lazarus is dead. And for your sake, I am glad I wasn't there, because this will give you another opportunity to believe in me. Come, let's go see him."

Jesus was like, y'all my boys and you still don't believe in me. SMH! Then one of the disciples named Thomas, nicknamed the "Twin", had the nerve to be smart mouth and say, "Let's go, too—and die with Jesus." Thomas got jokes. I know Jesus wanted to back hand Thomas aka Twin, but he probably just gave him a cold stare and John didn't want to write that part. John had already told us how Jesus flipped over the tables and benches in the temple and wouldn't let the people carry merchandise through the temple courts. One thing I know about Jesus and his disciples, they were not weak punks, they were straight up thugs! That's why Thomas' nickname was "Twin". Don't nobody call a real thug by his government name! We don't serve a weak God, know that. Jesus was the leader of the pack! (I'm just having a moment, excuse me).

When Jesus got to Bethany, He was told that Lazarus had been in the grave for four days already. Bethany was only about two miles down the road from Jerusalem. So, either the messenger was chilling for a few days before he gave Jesus the message or Mary and Martha waited until Lazarus had died to finally send a message to Jesus, their dear friend. We all know a body must be prepared for burial and the funeral and burial is not the same day as the death. It's at least two or three days later, and that's at the least. I do believe it was some deception of timing going on somewhere when the message got to Jesus, but it seems He nor the disciples addressed it and let it slide.

It was already a bunch of people trying to comfort and console Martha and Mary before Jesus even got to them. Basically, all those people already knew Lazarus had been dead for several days.

Somebody told Martha and Mary that Jesus was almost there and Martha, the feisty one, got up running to meet Jesus some ways out. Mary stayed in the house crying. Martha says to Jesus, "Lord, if you had been here my brother would not have died. But even now I know that God will give you whatever you ask." Sounds like she has lots of faith, right?

Jesus told her, "Your brother will rise again." And she says, "Yes, when everyone else rises on resurrection day." (All that faith she had just went straight up in dust with that comment right there.)

I know Jesus was much irritated at this point when He said to Martha, "I am the resurrection and the life. Those who believe in me, even though they die like everyone else, will live again. They are given eternal life for believing in me and will never perish. Do you believe this, Martha?"

"Yes Lord," she told Him. "I have always believed you are the Messiah, the son of God, the one who has come into the world from God." Then Martha left and went to Mary. She called Mary aside from the other mourners and told her, "The Teacher is here and wants to see you." And Mary immediately went to Him. I think Martha was lying because John did not say that Jesus told

Martha to go tell Mary to come to him. But he was letting us know where all this deception was probably coming from. Feisty Martha with the "wavering" faith.

Jesus stayed outside the village where Martha had met Him. When the people in the house that were trying to console Mary saw her leave so hastily, they thought she was going to Lazarus grave and to cry there. So, they followed her. When Mary finally got to Jesus she fell at his feet, (she just loves his feet). And she said the same thing that Martha said, "Lord, if you had been here, my brother would not have died." (I wonder where she got that thought from?)

But Jesus didn't get upset. When he saw how hard Mary was crying and how the other people with her were carrying on so emotionally and wailing and crying loudly, it moved him so deeply. All he could say was, "where have you put him?"

Jesus started crying. And then they came to the grave. It was a cave with a stone rolled in front of the entrance. Jesus told them to "Roll the stone aside." but Martha, the dead man's sister, (as John described her as if we didn't know. I think she had irritated him too at this point), said, "Lord by now the smell would be terrible because he has been dead for four days."

Jesus couldn't hold his irritation any longer with Martha, and he responded, "didn't I tell you that you will see God's glory if you believe?" Martha didn't say anything else after that. She already had sent word to Jesus to come because Lazarus was supposedly sick two days ago, but now she's saying Lazarus has been dead four days.

So, they rolled the stone away and Jesus looked up to heaven and he prayed to his heavenly father. "Father, thank you for hearing me. <u>You **always** hear me</u>, but I said it out loud for the sake of all these people standing here, *so they will believe you sent me*." (Did you catch that? That's an OG move right there!) Then Jesus shouted, "Lazarus come out!" And Lazarus came out, wrapped all up in his grave clothes and his face wrapped in a head cloth and Jesus told them to unwrap him and let him go!

I would like for you to take notice that there was some deception going on with the timing of Lazarus death. It appears the deception was coming from one of the sisters and it had to be Martha because Mary hardly said anything. And Martha was the one that said Lazarus had already been dead for four days. But Jesus had only got word a couple days prior that Lazarus was only sick. When He delayed the two days, He knew that Lazarus was dead. All He wanted to do was raise Lazarus from the dead, so that he could show the people the miracle of God working through Him, the Son of God.

Humans have a habit of either lying about time or using timing to deceive. Martha and Mary both said to Jesus, "If you had been here my brother would not have died." But Lazarus was already dead when they sent for Jesus. What sense does that make? No one really has the answers to why the timing is off here. We don't know and the focus was on the miracle so that the unbelievers could believe. But I want YOU to think about how humans are always off when it comes to time.

They show up to work late and blame it on the alarm clock. The doctor asks us how long we had a certain pain or ailment, and we don't know so we make up a time frame. The mechanic will ask us, how long has the car had this issue? And we don't know so we just make up a time frame. Stuff like that with time.

By paying attention to this story, I realized that if Jesus had left right away when the messenger came to him, Lazarus still would have been dead. And God is all knowing, so Jesus knew that, and he told the disciples that Lazarus was sleeping, and he was going to wake him. Jesus knew Lazarus was already dead. So why do you think Jesus really waited two more days before he went to Bethany? I believe it was so the disciples could come and witness the miracle because they needed to believe and Jesus knew they did not fully believe, and their behavior showed that. They said they didn't want to go because Jesus was almost killed when they were just there. And Thomas aka Twin had a smart remark about going. Jesus had to talk things out with the Disciples to get them to agree to go.

Therefore, in order for this miracle to have the effect that God intended for it to have, Jesus could not go right when the messenger told him to go. And it looked like to Martha and Mary and everybody else that if Jesus was there prior, then Lazarus would not have died. So, it looked like, and felt like to them, God showed up too late. Have you ever had a situation where it seemed like, to you, God showed up too late? He wasn't late, He was on time. Your timing, and your faith were off if you think God was too late. Just like Martha with her off timing and off faith.

The miracle that needed to happen, still happened. And it happened right on time. All of those that were supposed to witness the miracle were present. And God could not show up until it was so. That was the importance of God showing up on time. His time is not our time, **God's timing is aways on time**. The way we look at time and the way God looks at time is two different things.

We can't get time back. God's time is infinite. The time that we have to fulfill our Divine Purpose here on Earth, is numbered. God's time is infinite. We don't have time to waste. God's time is infinite.

If you were me and have known that you were created to write this very book since you were twelve years old, and you don't write it until you are in your 50's, does that mean that you were procrastinating and should have written it many years ago? No. When this book hits the market, is exactly when God says it is time.

Don't let anyone put you down or make you feel bad for when your time comes to walk in your purpose. Believe me, it's for the edification of God's Kingdom, and it's on time because God is an on-time God.

10

CHAPTER 10

WARM WATER

I do not like to drink warm water on a hot day. I don't like warm water on a cold day. I want a hot beverage on a cold day and a cold beverage on a hot day. Do not confuse warm water with room temperature bottled water, it is not the same thing.

Evidently God doesn't like lukewarm people because He said so in the Bible. He said to the Lukewarm church that they were neither cold nor hot, and He wishes for them to be either cold or hot. And since they are lukewarm, He will vomit them out His mouth. Vomit is nasty and foul smelling. I wouldn't want to be in God's vomit.

God continued telling them that they say they are rich and have become wealthy and have need of nothing. But they do not know that they are wretched, miserable, poor, blind, and naked. This is God the Son, aka Jesus, saying this in the book of Revelation. The original OG.

Another similar phrase is straddling the fence. No one can really sit on a fence comfortably with one leg on each side. That would hurt.

Being lukewarm and straddling the fence as a Christian is saying with your mouth that you are a Christian but how you live your life says otherwise. You have knowledge of God, may even go to church, but you have a foot in some ungodly activities in your life. God does not want us to be lukewarm or to straddle the fence. He wants us to serve Him wholeheartedly, or not at all. There is no grey area, no compromising in living your life as a Christian.

Being lukewarm and straddling the fence as an entrepreneur means you are not totally dedicated to achieving your dream. You say it with your mouth, but your actions show otherwise. You end up cutting yourself short that way. Therefore, there is no room for compromising, being lukewarm, or halfway pursuing your dreams, goals, and aspirations. You either are or you are not. And when you are, you must put your all into it to be successful at it. Since you don't know when your last breath will be, you must press hard towards your goals. I'm sure you would love to have a chance to enjoy the fruits of your labor while you are still living and breathing.

Another huge problem with being lukewarm or straddling the fence is the time and cost it will delete from your wealth building. Time and money are two components you should know you just cannot afford to waste. It's foolish to walk around as though you have got all the time in the world to build your wealth.

You need to be wholeheartedly into what it is that you are trying to accomplish. Being in between two totally different worlds is not a wise place to be. Make a choice to achieve your Divine destiny and give that decision your everything. It just isn't a good look to do otherwise. We are talking about building your storehouse and making boss moves; there is no room for delay.

Here is something else you need to consider: If you are looking flakey or unaccountable, no one will want to help you and won't take you seriously. A person that is not fully dedicated towards their goals and ambitions looks flakey and unpredictable to those who are. Serious people invest in serious people.

Remember when Jesus called them names? He said they think they are rich and have become wealthy and have need of nothing. But they do not know that they are wretched, miserable, poor, blind, and naked. When some people have accomplished a few things and have some money in their bank account, they forget to stay humble. They forget that it was God that opened doors for them and propelled them to where they are. They also can become complacent. These are behaviors and attitudes that cause you to lose what you have gained. Money will stop multiplying. Our blessings come from above, so when your cup is running over continue to give, stay humble, stay true to your calling, and still work hard. The more you get, the more you serve. The more you gain, the more you give. You have more to give more.

11

CHAPTER 11

MAKE IT PLAIN

When I've listened to famous and successful people talk about their journey towards walking in their gifts, they mention that they realized that we all have a purpose in this life. They came to this realization prior to walking in their purpose. Then they began to seek out what their purpose really was.

This realization is very important. Once you realize you were created for a specific purpose here on Earth, you then should be curious enough to seek out what that purpose is. Once you find out what that purpose is, you then should do all you can to fulfill that purpose.

This is important to becoming wealthy and successful because it is the actual **_act_** of following through with all determination to fulfill your purpose here on Earth, that brings true wealth and true success! You haven't accomplished wealth or success until you are indeed walking in what you were created to do. That's when blessings flow. I have many talents, but only the talents that I've used that were tied to my purpose have brought me blessings and success.

After finding out what your purpose is, you must set everything in motion to bring it into fruition. Writing it down and making it plain should be your first step. Write it down for you and then write it down for the purpose of others that may be of assistance to getting you to where you need to go with your vision.

Have you done your vision board yet? You should have a vision board, and/or a solid business plan done.

By making a vision board and/or business plan you have a visual guideline as to what it is you need to do and accomplish. The business plan is a good tool to use to show others that are in positions to lend you some type of help or advice. The vision board is to keep you focused.

Others take you more seriously when you have a business plan. When your vision is written down it is no longer just in your head. It is now in the atmosphere and easier to materialize. Once it hits the atmosphere it is closer to becoming a reality. As you look at it, and study it, you work towards manifesting it. You can't manifest what you don't see.

After your vision board or business plan is done, present it to God in prayer. Ask God to set everything in motion for the vision He has placed in you to materialize. In faith, start doing your part to work towards it and continue to thank God for His guidance and help. Proverbs 16:3 says, "Commit your work to the Lord, and your plans will be established." Believe and know that with all your faith your plans will be established and watch how God goes to work on your behalf.

12

CHAPTER 12

IT'S NO SECRET

I am grateful my maternal Grandmother said to me, "there is no secret to what God can do, what He has done for others He will do the same for you", because it framed my way of thinking. There really is no secret to wealth creating. Man tries to make it a secret because they don't want others to succeed, and that's jealousy and selfishness. The crab in the bucket mentality is not Godly at all. I have experienced being very generous and kind to certain people who I knew could offer help or information that I needed to succeed in something, and when I asked for help, it was not given. When that happens to you, you must see it for what it is and know that God will open every door necessary for your success regardless.

The keys to wealth building and personal success are written in the Word of God. It is not that it is a secret to man, the reason why it is not comprehended by all is because the Holy Spirit is necessary to have complete understanding of what the Bible is teaching. When the Holy Spirit dwells within you, the revelation of the Word of God is on a totally different level. It is miraculously a living Word, and it grows inside of your spirit, teaching, shaping, molding, and guiding you.

There are promises to us written in the Holy Bible. If you don't study the Bible, how will you know what is promised to you? And if you don't study as a believer filled with the Holy Spirit, you won't get full understanding of what God is promising His children. The first step is becoming a believer of God, and the second step is receiving the Holy Spirit. The third step is to study the Word of God diligently.

In 2 Corinthians Paul quotes the Old Testament saying, "Godly people give generously to the poor. Their good deeds will never be forgotten." This is in Psalm 112; a beautiful passage of how the Wealthy Believer lives his life. It is an example of how many people want to live their lives and how few have obtained it. The question is, how did those few get there? It's no secret.

They got there by applying generosity to their lifestyle and meeting the conditions God asked them to meet. (I have been sharing these conditions with you as you read this book). Some of the promises in the Bible come with stipulations or conditions such as to get that, you must first do this. This is what many people miss or omit. People are selfish and don't want to give, and when they do give, it's not their best and not done in the right spirit. Lack of generosity hurts you when it comes to wealth building. It holds up your blessings.

2 Corinthians 9:10-14

God is the One who gives seed to the farmer and then bread to eat. Meaning God will provide what you need to prosper and succeed. Every resource and every open-door, God will see to it that it happens for you. God will then multiply what He has given to you, and place in your direct path many opportunities for you to sow and give to others portions of what He has given to you. This is producing a great harvest of generosity in you. You will become and be seen as a very generous and good person.

You will receive even more from God because of how generous you are. When those in need receive your gifts of generosity, they will give praises and thanks to God!

Your generosity of giving out of the abundance of God will produce two good things: 1. The needs of God's people will be met. 2. The people will joyfully praise and thank God! God is overjoyed and well pleased by these results of your actions!

You will be glorifying God through your giving. Because of this and your obedience, God will keep on giving to you more and more and more. The people that you give to will not only be thankful and praise God, but they will pray for you because you were so kind and helpful to them. They will pray for your safety, for your protection, and for you to continue to be blessed! This will activate the Heavens to move even more on your behalf and you receive even more blessings on top of what God was already doing for you!

Keep in mind that while all this is taking place you will have enemies that don't want to see you prosper. The Bible tells you that God helps you conquer your enemies. Your giving is sowing seeds, seeds that ensure your protection from your enemies. People begin to pray for you and your loved ones. Do you see what I am telling you here? Your giving is not only producing more for you to give, but it is also activating the prayers of the saints for your protection. It is ensuring that the angelic forces assigned to you are fighting battles on your behalf and you are conquering your enemies in the process. The Kingdom of Heaven suffers violence, and the violent take it by force. Mathew 11:12. Prayer's lead to victory. Your life is a constant battlefield, spiritually and naturally, and you are the general of your Army. How you live your life is also a reflection of how your battles will be fought and won. Victorious battles bring prosperity. In the Bible we see how God's people have victorious battles, and they always bring back the riches of those they conquered.

Every battle that you go through in life and overcome, you will walk away enriched, enlightened, and richer than you were prior to that battle. And your opponent is left defeated.

Give generously during your wealth building. The gain you will receive from your generosity cannot be measured.

I know I have been talking a lot about giving, in different sections of the book, but it's a key component and the component that is the hardest to do. I can't stress it enough. People are selfish when it comes to giving to others.

In Psalms 112, we see that wealthy believers are happy people, and they will be remembered for the good deeds they do. They happily enjoy doing the commands of God. They happily meet the conditions needed to receive the promises of God. Their children are successful wherever they go and with whatever they do. Their entire generation of offspring are blessed because of their obedience. They are generous, compassionate, and righteous people. (These are conditions that you must meet). Everything will go well for generous people who lend freely and conduct their business fairly. Evil circumstances will not overcome them. (There will be a lot of prayers going up on your behalf).

Righteous people will long be remembered. They do not fear bad news because they trust solely in God to care for them. They are confident and fearless and can face their enemies triumphantly. They give generously to those in need. They have great influence and are honored.

It infuriates and angers the wicked to see the believers blessed like this. Everything the wicked tries to do to this believer, will fail.

Follow the formula to success given to you in the Word of God and prosper in your purpose. There is no secret to what God can do, what He has done for others He will do the same for you.

13

CHAPTER 13

DEADLINES

For some reason I don't like deadlines. It's so many positive things about setting deadlines and meeting them. But with doing my own work, I don't set deadlines and then I find out that something else had to take place in my life to add to the writing and I was glad I waited. This is not the case for everything and everyone. But I will tell you that the Bible tells us that your grapes will not shrivel before they are ripe, and everything has a season and a time.

You have to be in tune with the Holy Spirit to know your season and the right timing to walk in your particular purpose successfully. If you don't set a deadline, make sure that you are not procrastinating or being lazy. Deadlines allow us time to get work done without having to cram everything in at once. Being able to take your time to deliver a product of excellence is what is of importance.

Another thing that is good to do is to set timetables. You can give yourself a certain number of days to complete each step and continue to proceed that way.

Make sure your work is done in a timely manner but is still good, acceptable, and darn near perfect! I think we should always strive for perfection. To achieve that level of perfection, deadlines and timetables need to be realistic amounts of time and allow for mistakes and corrections.

Prioritize your life by keeping to a schedule. Schedule in family time, eating breaks, exercising, adequate amounts of sleep, leisure and selfcare time, work, working on pursuing your calling, etc. This makes it less stressful for you to achieve your wealth building goals. When you become stressed trying to pursue your purpose it is easy for you to become less motivated and even give up.

The trials and tribulations are going to come through all of this, and you want to be as little stressed as possible to be better equipped to handle them.

14

CHAPTER 14

FIXING YOUR FINANCES

I strongly feel we need to be good stewards of what God has blessed us with. Especially what He gives to us financially. Part of that is being a tither, but there are a lot of other ways as well. I believe it shows God our financial gratitude and we are blessed even more so, because we are so grateful and responsible with what He has given us.

"The person who is trustworthy in very small matters is also trustworthy in great ones; and the person who is dishonest in very small matters is also dishonest in great ones. If then you have not been faithful with the dishonest wealth, who will entrust to you the true riches?" Luke 16:10-11.

Your moral standards and integrity are displayed in how you manage your money matters, believe it or not. That explains why givers are so praised and have such high favor with man and God. Takers are looked down upon, as they should be. Being stingy and frugal with your money is not a good sign of one with good integrity. It is not saving; it is being selfish. If a person steals something small, they will be dishonest with something big as well. If you want to know about someone's character, look at how they handle their money and money matters.

When a person takes or robs from another source, they create a lack in their own life. What they are putting out will return to them. You will see a lack in their home, business affairs, etc. Wealth acquired dishonestly is not success. It comes with sleepless nights, fear of discovery, illness, and a guilty conscience. It separates the person from God and makes them a cold-hearted person.

It's not wise to spend more than you earn. You can never get ahead that way. Don't live in the moment, vacationing, buying cars, boats, and the latest new gadgets. A sudden tragic or unexpected life circumstance may floor you. Like a death in the family, serious illness, divorce, loss of a job, forced retirement. You need to be financially prepared for those sudden life tragedies.

Living beyond your means with too large of a house payment, lavish vacations, too many credit cards that are maxed out is also not wise. People do this and then wonder why it is hard to live on what they are making as income.

Everyone should have a cushion fund, or emergency savings. It should be 3 to 6 times your basic monthly expenses, including mortgage or rent, groceries, health insurance, car insurance, credit card payments, utilities, phone, gasoline, car payment, and childcare, to name a few.

Don't mix emergency funds with what you are saving for. Save in a special separate account for trips and holidays. Use automatic deposits into your emergency account and special accounts.

Pay off your mortgage! Nothing is more refreshing than a paid off home when you finally move into retirement years. Avoid home equity loans. They add years to pay for your home and increase your mortgage payments. You can't pay off the mortgage if you continue to borrow against it. It's nice to know that you have somewhere to live, that you own, if you must be on a fixed income. You will still have utilities, and many people still will have to pay property taxes, and not having mortgage debt on your home will be a huge weight off your shoulders!

As you are paying off your home, your equity builds on the home. Homeowners have more financial freedom when they let their home equity build. It also serves as a second emergency fund. You can add an extra $100 or $200 a month to reduce the principal of the loan or pay an extra payment a year. By doing this you will reduce the amount of interest you pay.

A home is an investment. It appreciates in value. I believe in investing in buying a home over renting but buy a home you can afford. Rent never stops, and eventually a mortgage will be paid off and will stop. Keep in mind the larger a house you have, the larger your expenses will be that comes along with that house. (Heat, electricity, maintenance, repairs, furniture, HOA dues are higher in more expensive areas). It will drain your wallet.

Eliminate debt. Having debt creates worry and ties up financial freedom. Too many bills and not enough money to pay for them creates anger. People drive with road rage, argue in the grocery store, all kinds of things because they are mad, they just got their paycheck and it's gone already to the bills. People deep in debt are unhappy people. Start with the smallest credit card or loan and begin to pay it off or pay off high interest debts first. Don't create more debt. Pay your bills on time so you don't incur unnecessary late fees.

There is good debt and bad debt. Any debt that increases in value is considered good debt. A debt that you take on to generate more income or build your net worth is good debt. Examples of good debt are your home, rental property or real estate, school loan, business loan, etc. It is still debt that is owed and needs to be paid off.

Bad debt is debt that does not go up in value and/or does not generate income. Borrowing money to purchase a car is actually bad debt. The car depreciates in value, and you will more than likely owe more on the car than the car is worth. Or put more money into the car than the car is worth. Don't purchase brand new cars to try to offset the amount of this debt. Buy used vehicles. Expensive clothes, shoes, furniture, is bad debt, especially if you are borrowing or using high interest credit cards to pay for them. Try to pay cash for these items. You must decide what is good debt and what is bad debt in your personal purchasing strategies and stay away from bad debt as much as possible.

Cut back on your spending and track your spending habits. Make a budget plan to live by for each month or each paycheck. By tracking your spending habits, you will see where you have room to cut back and save in that area.

You will be surprised at how much you spend in certain areas.

Save as much as you can. Put the money you save from cutting back into a separate savings account. Make a savings account for your children as well.

Work on improving your credit score. Get a copy of your credit report and pay off debts owed and make sure everything is correct on your credit report. Pay all your bills on time and this will help your credit score as well.

File your taxes and don't cheat on them because it will catch up with you. Plan for your retirement. Invest, save, whatever you need to do, make sure you are preparing for retirement and the age that you can no longer work and make money.

15

CHAPTER 15

RICH THOUGHTS

Just like it is your right to be happy, it is your right to be rich. In whatever way rich means to you, you have a right to achieve it. Whatever luxury you want, you have a right to own it. Whatever businesses you want, you have a right to own them and prosper from them. No one should make you feel bad because you dream and achieve something big. Feel good about that because it is your right! Just be wise about it.

Having prosperity makes life easier. Prosperity coupled with mature handling of your money matters makes life exciting, enjoyable, and gives you freedom and access to things the average individual will never have.

When you have a surplus of money it is not just a sign of wealth, it is a sign of health. Poverty is a state of sickness. It is not healthy to live in poor conditions and not want more for yourself and your children. That is a sick thought, sick way of thinking, and sick way of living. Those in poverty don't get the best this world has to offer. They don't get the best healthcare, they don't get the best travel options, they don't get the best education, they don't even get the best food to eat. To eat healthily can become expensive, and they don't have the best because they don't have the means to pay for the best. It is not healthy to live in poverty or to have a poverty mentality. To be able to have a surplus of riches is to be economically healthy.

When the state of the country you live in has taken an economic downward spiral, it does not affect the rich. The rich have savings for those times. Food and gas prices elevate but economically healthy people have the means to purchase what they need, and the higher pricing does not affect them negatively.

The rich remain rich because they think rich. These are people that understand money will flow to them in abundance regardless of any outside factors. When you think like this, you attract what you think. When you know that you are here on this Earth to live abundantly, and it is your right to always have that overflow of abundance, you will never be poor. No one controls your way of thinking but you, so if you have financial lack it is because of your own way of thinking. You have the right to be rich and you need to think rich thoughts and pursue rich means. You need to know in your mind without any doubt that you will always have an overflow of wealth and riches.

Some people walk around saying they do not believe in prosperity teaching. They think it's a sin to have the luxury of this world. If they want to live in lack, let them. They think that way so let them live that way. You can't control anyone's way of thinking but your own. If you don't believe what they are saying is true, don't entertain such negative thoughts. Think rich thoughts and wisely go get and enjoy the riches of this world!

Do not say things like, "I am broke", "I am poor", "I have no money". That is a poverty mindset and what you think and say will be what you get: poverty. Empty pockets. You should believe that $1 in YOUR pocket is equivalent to $1000 in this world, because that's just who YOU are! You can manifest riches in your life because you have the God given power within you to do so.

The vision board with all that you plan to achieve is a visual that will help you develop this way of thinking. Visualizing yourself enjoying the luxuries that you want will help motivate you to work towards getting them. It is also putting out into the universe what you are attracting and manifesting to come to you. That is your power, but you must tap into it. What you are attracting will begin to seek you out and you will eventually have what you are visualizing. But you must do the work to get it. You must use your Divine Purpose to create this type of riches. It is like payment for your doing what you were created to do.

Let's say you work for a corporation, and you have the desire to become president of the corporation. That's your purpose and it's nothing wrong with that, God has a reason that He wants you to have that position and that's why it is heavy on your heart. If you are always complaining about the position, you currently have, or complaining about your current pay, you can bet you will never be president of that corporation. You may end up losing the job because you weren't thankful for the small things you had. You cannot think or speak negatively about this job or corporation at all. Cast down such thoughts and train your mind to only see the good, and to see why you are needed there, and the awesome difference you will make even in your current position. And feel good about that.

You must make your vision board with you in the position that you want and include the wonderful changes and benefits you will bring to this corporation on the vision board. If you want a new home and car once in the position, include that on the vision board as well. Then be thankful for the position and pay that you do have. Strive to only speak positive about the corporation because one day you will be president of it! Thank God daily that He is opening all the right doors and sending all the right people in your direct path to get you to the position of president. It is in fact, God's will for you to have this position, so He will make it happen for you if you do the necessary steps to achieve it. This is an example of the law of action and reaction. The action was your thoughts, and the reaction was the universe manifesting your thoughts.

"Whatever things are true, whatever things are noble, whatever things are just, whatever things are pure, whatever things are lovely, whatever things are of good report, if there is any virtue and if there is anything praiseworthy, meditate on these things." Philippians 4:8. Walking and living in your Divine Purpose and living a happy, economically fulfilling life is honorable, noble, lovely, and praiseworthy. Think on them, meditate on them all day long. Let your every move be towards walking in your calling and building the wealth you desire.

A workman is worthy of his hire, it says in Luke 10:7. When people want to give to you and support you, do not refuse it. It is the universe carrying out the wealth that you are manifesting. Even if it's words of wisdom, listen to them, and receive that wealth of knowledge. The work that you put in to achieve your goals will pay off because you are worthy to be paid for it. Understand wealth is not limited to a paycheck.

God is all knowing; God is omniscient. Which means He knows how our life will end up. He knows the end result of us walking and working in our calling. It's not a mystery, He shows it to you. Know that when you are thinking big and seeing a much larger picture than where your life is now, that's God showing you what the end should be. Believe that can happen and put that vision on paper. Keep those thoughts in the forefront of your mind because they came from God above.

It doesn't matter where you are today or what you are today. Because tomorrow you will be much greater and that is the reason you are still living and breathing. It's a testimony to share where you have come from and what you had to go through to get to the mountain top. It was not coincidence, it was Divinely ordained, everything you went through good and bad, had a reason attached to it. It will propel you towards your greatness and help others in the process. Don't even look at your experiences negatively, find the lessons in them and educate others with those lessons. You wouldn't have learned those lessons if you didn't go through those experiences. Give back by sharing your testimonies and helping others to avoid the same mistakes. Always give.

16

CHAPTER 16

FROM BAD TO GOOD

Chris Brown says in one of his songs, "I get what you make in 10 years, in 2 days." And that is the difference in a person walking in their purpose and a person that doesn't know their purpose and is content slaving for hours for a small paycheck. Or they may know their purpose but aren't pursuing their purpose or they have an unproductive thought process.

The mind is full of ideas. Everyone has some thoughts towards ideas but it's up to them to pursue those ideas and turn them into wealth. You can still have a lack of wealth although you have many ideas. If you are an envious person, a liar and deceptive person, a person that steals and has low integrity, a selfish and greedy person, a person that tries to get money in unrighteous and unlawful ways, then the wealth will not remain with you. It will run through you like diarrhea.

This is so because the wealth of the unrighteous is stored up for the righteous. Proverbs 13:22. Wealth is going to gravitate to who it belongs to. Therefore, you see people who have obtained money unlawfully have nothing to show for it. Or those whose heart is not righteous have no riches although they work and have ideas.

For this reason, it isn't necessary to worry about people who are obtaining wealth on any scale while their heart is not right. That person is using their thoughts negatively and will attract back the negativity that they put out on a greater scale. The universe handles those types of matters in its time. Keep your mind free from that concern, only thinking on positive things so you are not affected by negative thinking as well. When you ponder on such matters it creates negative thoughts within you.

"And we know that all things work together for good to those who love God, to those who are the called according to His purpose." Romans 8:28. Although we have the right to be happy, God is not concerned with making us happy. God is concerned with getting His purpose fulfilled. That also includes when the person walking in their purpose comes against opposition, God will turn that bad situation around and make it a good situation for that person. This is not so for the unrighteous.

The unrighteous can be walking in their purpose and collecting wealth, but it will not remain, and they have no advocate to turn their adversities from bad to good. They have no Savior. So, they eventually end up going downhill because there is no help for them. God is our very present help. God is always there for us; we are never without Him and his provisions. The unrighteous do not have this help at all. "God is our refuge and strength, A very present help in trouble". Psalm 46:1 NKJV. God is there to deliver us from the snare of the enemy in times of trouble because we must continue to fulfill our purpose for Him, and because we love, worship, praise Him, and have an intimate relationship with Him. Everything that we do will prosper.

17

CHAPTER 17

LET'S TALK 23

Sugarology 23

Let us look at what Psalms 23 means to me:

1 My name is Sugar aka Vikki aka J-Chill, and I love the Lord. My faith in God is everything to me and I try with all my humanly might to do what's right in the sight of God. God is a Shepherd, and I am His precious lamb. I **completely** depend on Him, and He gives me everything I need. I lack nothing.

2 He lets me rest in safe surroundings and comfortable atmospheres. I don't have to look for these places because He directs my path and leads me to them. I walk in peace, and I reside in peaceful places that God provides for me.

3 Sometimes I do get tired and become weary with the trials of my life, but then my Shepherd breathes new strength into my nostrils, and I am able to continue this journey without becoming sick with depression, low self-esteem, addictions, or anything that will cause me to stumble. Instead, He gives me the will power I need to continue on the path of righteousness. I make it clear to all that it is not I that has the strength to press on but rather

it is the Holy Spirit that lives within me that guides me and gives me all the strength I need without me asking.

4 Even when evil is lurking all around me and people are trying hard to cause me to fail or fall, I walk with confidence, and I remain in my confidence because I know I am not walking alone. Others may try to slay or kill me, but I am not afraid because my God fights and defeats my every battle. When storms are raging in my life, I am calm and comforted by the Comforter who ensures my constant protection.

5 The wonderful thing about how God provides everything that I need, is that it is not a secret and done openly. Everyone who has wronged me or tried to do me wrong can clearly see their attempts have failed and God is still elevating me. It is not a secret that I am a child of the Most High King and He has anointed me with supernatural power. I am so tremendously blessed that others look on in bewilderment and can't understand how it is so.

6 As long as I continue to walk this path of righteousness with my Heavenly Father, I can rest assured that His goodness and unfailing love will continue to provide everything I need and more. I don't have to wait for it or look for it because He will follow me with his goodness for the rest of my life. This will be how I live, move, and have my being forever.

Psalms 23 (A psalm of David)

1 The Lord is my shepherd; I have all that I need. 2 He lets me rest in green meadows; he leads me beside peaceful streams. 3 He renews my strength. He guides me along right paths, bringing honor to his name. 4 Even when I walk through the darkest valley, I will not be afraid, for you are close beside me. Your rod and your staff protect and comfort me. 5 You prepare a feast for me in the presence of my enemies. You honor me by anointing my head with oil. My cup overflows with blessings. 6 Surely your goodness and unfailing love will pursue me all the days of my life, and I will live in the house of the Lord forever.

Acts 17:28

For in Him we live and in Him we move, and it is in Him with whom we exist. (That is, in Him we have our being), as even some of your own poets have said, 'For we also are His children.'

Write your very own Psalms 23 and keep it where you can read it often.

18

CHAPTER 18

WHERE IS THE CONFUSION

Where there is confusion and where there is chaos, God is not the author. Every atmosphere that God provides for us is one of peace and certainty. Dark and demonic forces walk this Earth and beyond and they are real.

Consider the fact that every human being is a host for another living entity. You are a natural vessel that host other living organisms. Most of these organisms include bacteria, viruses, fungi, yeast, parasites, and spirits, although spirits are not naturally living, they are spiritually living.

For the most part these living organisms stay with you from birth until death and they help you grow. If they become unbalanced or overpopulated, then you will get physically sick and need an antibiotic to kill some of them off. If you have an unbalanced or overpopulation of spirit entities within you, you are considered to be sin sick. Then you will need to heal spiritually by rebuking the unwanted spirits that you are hosting.

Upon the understanding that you are a host for different microbes, you should not be confused, shocked, or ignorant to the fact that you are a host for different spirits as well.

I'm sure the dark forces of this world would rather you be confused in this area so they can continue to reside within you and cause discourse in your life. But the Holy Spirit wants you to be knowledgeable in this area and live free of chaos and confusion. Free from being in a sin sick state because you are a host to dark spiritual beings.

Let's look at Mathew 8 starting with the 28th verse. Jesus was walking along the countryside minding his business and enjoying His stroll. Out jumps not one, but two, demon possessed men. Right there you see you can be minding your business and living your life and all of a sudden here comes Satan's demons living within another person or persons trying to cause chaos, fear, and turmoil within your life. You can also see that it is common for people to be a host for demonic spirits. Don't be oblivious to that fact.

These two men hosting demonic spirits, jumped out of a tomb in a fierce, mean, nasty, confrontational way at Jesus. The tomb represents a dark place in which they live. Depression, anger, selfishness, jealousy, unforgiveness, maliciousness, self-centeredness, bitterness, vengefulness, vindictiveness, animosity, hostility, hatred, are some examples of dark places in which people live. These men were so earthly scary and uncontrollably wild within the dark place in which they lived, that nobody wanted to have any dealings with them for fear of their lives. And take note that if they didn't know who anybody else was, they knew exactly who Jesus was.

Think about people who know exactly who God is but continue to live in their sin, and now you know why it is so. They are hosting demonic spirits and that is why they continue in their sin. These spirits know who Jesus is.

Even if the men in this Biblical story did not personally know Jesus, the demonic spirits that lived within them knew exactly who Jesus was and knew his position in the Heavenly Kingdom. They have seen Him many times before in the Heavenly realm when they were angels, before being casted out with Satan for their rebellion against God.

They biggest key point is they knew Jesus had the power to torment them and to cast them out of their human hosts. Which is exactly what Jesus did.

The people who saw this ran into the city telling others what they just saw. It appears they were running with excitement and happy that the sin sick can be healed of demonic inhabitants. But this was not so, they didn't like the actions of Jesus at all. And what happened as a result was others came running from the city to see Jesus, bothering Him while he was trying to have some peace and quiet on his stroll. These people told Jesus to get out of their town! They did not want Him there casting out the demonic spirits that they host! We should not be confused or bewildered by this fact either.

People who live in darkness, people who are infested with demonic spirits, do not want to be tormented by the bright light that those who are host for the Holy Spirit bring. These people want to continue to live in their sin sick state. They even feel that this way of life is a good way of life. And just like those demon possessed men would jump out at people and cause chaos in their lives, and scare them, and bring fear upon them, this is what they will do to you in your everyday life. But with the power invested in you through the Holy Spirit, you can rebuke them, and you can overcome any chaos and confusion that these types of infested people bring to your life.

It is wise to realize that you are a host for other living organisms. And spirits are real, and they inhabit people as well. How you address that fact within your own life will also be a factor in how you become successful in achieving your Divine purpose.

Being that the purpose of demonic spirits is to destroy whoever or whatever they inhibit, when they are cast out of their present host, they will look for another host to go to and try to destroy it instead. These demons asked Jesus to send them to a herd of pigs. It would appear to the reader that Jesus caused these herd of pigs to run into the sea and die so that they could kill the demonic spirits that were just cast into them. But this is not what happened at all because spirits don't die. The demonic spirits drove the herd of swine into the sea so that they could destroy every one of those pigs that they were now inhabiting. Because the whole purpose of demonic spirits is to destroy who or whatever they inhabitant.

Therefore, if you are a host for any demonic spirit or spirits, understand the purpose is to destroy you. You will not reach Divine wealth in such a sin sick state. You will be destroyed eventually.

Think about the way that you live your life. If you are a habitual liar, if you are a continuous adulterer, If you are an alcoholic, drug addict, or even sex and porn addict, if you are a murderer and have a lot of hate in your heart, if you do not honor and respect your mother and your father, if you are worshiping anything other than God or any person other than God, these and ungodly actions like these, are controlling you because you are a host for that particular demonic spirit. Eventually you will be destroyed unless you cast them out and fill yourself with the goodness of the Holy Spirit. You will not achieve the greatness that God created you to achieve. And that is the plan of Satan for your life.

CHAPTER 19

HOW TO KICK BUTT

It is our natural instinct to want to punch and fight someone that has wronged us in some way. We need to change this way of thinking into a supernatural way of thinking.

Become an extra ordinary thinker as you grow into becoming an extraordinary person.

Ephesians 6:10-20 teaches us how to fight in a supernaturally extraordinary way. I had to learn this myself. I grew up physically fighting at any given moment. If I was opposed, I would physically fight. I had to learn on my own, through the teachings in the Bible how to effectively fight and win.

We know that it is demonic spirits within people that come against us. It appears to be the person because the person is the host, the carrying vessel. But when we retaliate, we are retaliating against the person instead of the demonic spirit. You cannot physically fight a spiritual entity. Therefore, we're only creating a bigger situation for ourselves because the demonic spirit is winning when we physically retaliate. In Ephesians chapter 6 we are educated in the fact that we must put on a whole armor of God in order to fight against the devil and his tactics spiritually. We can't put on half the armor, or some of the armor, we must put on the entire armor of God. Experience taught me this very well.

The Word of God goes on to tell us that this fight is not against the flesh and blood or the individual that the demonic host is speaking through or opposing us through, but instead we are wrestling against the rulers in the darkness of this age that exists in this day and time.

Imagine yourself mad and angry at someone else and you punch a hole in the wall, or bust the windows out of a car, or break your cell phone, or physically assault that person and you end up in jail. What good have you accomplished by doing this? None.

If it is not wise to fight in a physical way, then what is the right way to fight? You know that it's a battle just to survive in this world. And a battle is merely a fight. If you are wrestling against the principalities and powers that are spiritual, nothing physical that you do will win the battle. You must fight spiritual beings in a spiritual manner if you want to win the fight.

The first thing you must do when met with demonic opposition, is not act on impulse, but be still and stand. Hold your ground, the Chosen are not cowards.

You need to be strong in truth. Satan comes with lies, but you can stand on truth. You must avoid and put off lying. You must instead be a person of integrity, high morals, and standards, and be in a right position with God. Know the correct Word of God to combat any lie or wrong action done against you.

Satan will often use relationships and people to attack your heart with negative emotions, to insult your intelligence and to diminish your self-worth. But if you remember who God says you are, those things will have minimal to no effect on you. It's important to stay strong in that area.

You must have strong faith. This opens the door for the angelic beings on your side to fight the demonic beings opposing you. That was the example of Jesus casting out the demons. Whether it's casting them out of the host or away from harming you. The battle will be fought and won on your behalf.

Resist evil temptations by staying strong in the Word and prayer. Falling prey to the enemy in any way will only hold up your personal mission.

Never doubt God. Cast away all thoughts of doubt when it comes to who you are in Christ and fulfilling your purpose that God created you to do. The enemy will try to make you doubt God. Don't do that. Focus on the end result of your mission and press towards accomplishing that.

The biggest thing to remember is to always pray. Pray without ceasing all day long. Whatever the situation may be on an everyday basis, stay in prayer about each different situation as they spring up. Pray for other people that are going through tough times as well.

I know it sounds like you can't win against opposing forces by doing this. As strange as it may seem, this is how you successfully kick butt in life. This is the winning formula.

20

CHAPTER 20

PRAYER

"... the earnest (heartfelt, never ceasing, continued) prayer of a righteous man makes tremendous power available [being dynamic in its working}." James 5:16.

If you continue to read beyond that verse, you will learn that Elijah was a human being with a nature such as we have {with feelings, affections, and a constitution like ours}; And he prayed earnestly for it not to rain, and no rain fell on the earth for three years and six months. And {then} he prayed again, and the heavens supplied rain, and the land produced its crops {as usual}.

God wants us to know that we are no different from Elijah in our nature, the same power Elijah had in biblical days, we still have in us today *if we believe*. Just to let you know how human this powerful, respected prophet named Elijah was, he suffered from depression, isolation, and loneliness. He fled in fear when his life was sought after, and he was introverted and worked alone. Jesus said that Elijah was badly mistreated, and the Bible mentions he was mistreated by other believers as well. Elijah was a man of great power who restored a dead child to his mother, prayed rain away and prayed the rain back when it was needed, and he appeared with Moses to talk with Jesus before Jesus's crucifixion. Elijah was highly favored by God; he responded to and answered his calling and had a direct relationship with God. This is how powerful you should be as a Chosen believer.

Prayer is another highly important ingredient in wealth building, and I am about to explain to you why it is so and how it should be done.

It is the right of a believer to receive answers to their prayers. As a believer, God has granted us the right to ask anything of Him and to be assured that He hears our prayers. In the book of John 16, Jesus tells us to ask for what we want, and we will receive. If you have not, it is because you ask not, or you are not asking in prayer correctly so that your prayers will be heard and answered.

Your prayer life must be one that includes praying without ceasing in order to enjoy the fullness of joy on earth today. It is something seriously wrong if you have been a Christian for years and have unanswered prayers. If you claim to be a child of God but have unanswered prayers, you are ineffectual to the body of Christ. It should never be that a person is a child of God but never have their prayers answered. Every believer should have the testimony of how God answers their prayers. Every Christian should be able to say they frequently experience God answering their prayers. This is a basic experience of being a believer. If God has not answered your prayers in a long time, then you should examine yourself because something is wrong with that picture.

Prayer has a purpose. Prayer is not to be just saying eloquent words or to be confused with giving praise. Prayer is conversation with God in a manner that we are making our requests known to God, and God is honoring our request in return because he loves us just that much. The purpose of prayer is to be answered.

Why pray if you know God will not answer? Makes no sense at all. God is who you believe in, and you should know that God will answer your prayers.

Pray until you get your answer from God. The Bible says pray without ceasing. Keep asking God until you get the results you are praying for. Prayer sounds easy to learn to do but it must not be as easy as it sounds since many people don't pray, don't know how to pray, or don't pray effectively. Prayer is simple yet profound at the same time. Prayer is so profound that some never learn to do it well after partaking in it all their Christian lives. Prayer is so simple to those who know how to effectively pray. To walk in your Divine Destiny, it is essential that you learn how to pray so you will receive answers from God for your prayers. You will need to ask God to open doors for you, fight on your behalf, give you the wealth building materials you need, etc.

When you pray you should be petitioning God for something. Making your requests known to God. Not just praying vain repetitions and not expecting answers from God. Your request should not be vague but clear and precise. You should be able to pinpoint exactly what it is that you are asking God for. If you can't, then your so-called prayer held no value and was bouncing off the ceiling. Praying a prayer that is vague and empty in content with no clear purpose, is like knocking on wall. Accomplishes nothing. God says, "Knock and the door shall be opened to you". If you are knocking on the wall there is no door for God to open. But if you knock on the door, God will surely answer the door and open it for you! God says, "Seek and you shall find". Therefore, when God answers the door, you can walk right in and find the answer you were looking for. "The fervent effectual prayers of the righteous avails much". James 5:16.

God wants to know specifically what you want and exactly what you are asking for. This is the only way He will grant your request. The definition of "ask" is to say something to obtain an answer or some information; request (someone) to do or give something. The definition of "prayer" is a solemn request for help addressed to God; an earnest hope or wish. You must ask specifically for what you want from God in prayer. This is what it means to knock, and the door shall be open to you and to seek and you shall find. When you go to a restaurant you have to give your specific order and specifically how you want your food prepared, and watch this, YOU EXPECT TO RECEIVE EXACTLY WHAT YOU ORDERED, PREPARED EXACTLY HOW YOU INSTRUCTED. This is how you should pray to God. Asking for what you want and expecting Him to give it to you.

Believers hinder themselves because they do not ask God in prayer for what they want, or they ask not really expecting answered prayer or with doubt that they will receive what they are asking for.

James 4:2-3 says, "You want what you don't have, so you scheme and kill to get it. You are jealous for what others have, and you can't possess it, so you fight and quarrel to take it away from them. And yet the reason you don't have what you want is that you don't ask God for it. And even when you do ask, you don't get it because your whole motive is wrong—you want only what will give you pleasure."

This is so true about the world we live in. People kill, steal, rob and scheme to get what others have because they cannot get it on their own. The whole reason they don't have it is because they are not in right standing with God and/or they don't ask God for it. And if they do ask, they are not going to get it because it is not God's will for them to have it because their motives behind why they want it are not godly or pure.

Which brings us to the second point of prayer. You want God to answer your prayers because there will be times of trouble, and you will need God to deliver you from that evil attack against you. If you don't know how to pray for exactly what you want in times of peace, then when trouble comes you still won't know how to pray for what you need God to do on your behalf. Then you are just left stuck in a sticky situation that God could have delivered you from had you asked. He wants us to ask and know He will answer, in other words, ask for exactly what we want in assured faith. You need specific prayers to deal with specific problems.

The third point is your prayers and what you are asking for need to be in God's will. It is foolish to ask God for unnecessary things out of your own lusts and greed. He isn't hearing that foolishness.

In Psalm 66:18 it says if your heart is not right, God does not hear your prayers. Are you practicing any type of sin in your life? That is the barrier between you and God and the reason why God is not hearing and answering your prayers. This is my fourth point.

To regard iniquity in your heart means you are practicing a sin and don't want to let go of it. Like maybe sleeping with someone and one or both of you are married to someone else, yet you do not want to stop sleeping with this person and you continue to partition God in prayer for what you want. God is not entertaining your prayer. Your prayers are not going past the ceiling. I am sorry to break the bad news to you, but it is what it is. When Jesus was on the cross, He took on all our sins, and you know what God did? God turned away from Jesus, disconnected from His only son because of the sin Jesus now carried. Jesus cried out to His father because Jesus had never been without the presence of God, and He was lost and hurt without God in His life at this terribly painful and crucial time in His life. God didn't answer Jesus either, because the sin was a barrier, like a huge thick stone wall where you can't see over it or hear through it. Sin in our lives prevents us from having answered prayer.

If you are reluctant and unwilling to let go of the sin in your life, this hinders God from answering your prayers. Even if the sin is not in your actions but in your heart, the Lord will not hear you when you pray. All sins need to be acknowledged and let go of in actions as well as in your heart so you will have answered prayers. Even if it is just one sin, for example, like lying, no matter how small you think the lie is, it's still a sinful act. It will prevent your prayers from being answered. Not honoring a parent is a sin, and so many people have unpleasant and disrespectful thoughts and actions towards their parent or parents and wonder why their life is out of whack and God is not answering their prayers. There is no justification for why you participate in a sin when God says don't do it and you do it anyway. It's no need to expect answered prayer when your heart is sinful. God is not going to hear your prayer until you genuinely repent and cast away that sin totally from within you.

My fifth point is having faith when you ask God for something. Faith is essential. Faith is beyond necessary. Without faith, prayer is useless. Why would someone ask God for something and not believe that He will give it to them? Again, senseless, but people do it.

You must pray and believe that you have already received what you are asking God for. That's what faith is; the substance of things hoped for, and the evidence of things not seen. You cannot pray and say to yourself I will eventually get this; you must pray and know that it is already done. You must pray with the assurance that it is already done, and God has already answered your prayer before you even prayed it. You can just start thanking God because you know He has already answered your prayer. If you are sick, you cannot say to yourself I believe God *will* heal me from my sickness. This way of thinking and praying is not faith because it leaves room for doubt. You cannot have any doubt and expect results. You must know and believe without a doubt that you are already healed, and your prayers have already been answered. You must say to yourself, I am healed, Amen.

In wealth building, we need God to hear and answer our prayers. We need to have no doubt and know we will have answered prayers.

21

CHAPTER 21

GOD CAN

Entertain the thought that when we doubt God, it may disappoint Him or even upset Him in some instances. As humans, when our very own loved ones doubt us or don't believe in us, it's hurtful. God who is our provider and everything else we need Him to be, has shown us His power and for us to come to him doubting that He will do what we need Him to do is insulting. Why believe in God if you doubt His power?

There is a story in the Bible that demonstrates that doubting God really does upset Him. Like I said before, Jesus was not a weak punk like some people want to make Him out to be. Who would serve a weak King? Not I.

We can find this story in Mark 9:14-29. It is the story of Jesus healing a demon possessed boy.

One day Jesus, Peter, James, and John were walking down a mountain and at the bottom of the mountain they found a great crowd of people surrounding the other disciples and some religious law teachers arguing with the disciples. When the crowd saw Jesus, they were amazed and watched Him in awe as he approached them. When He got close, they ran to greet Him. Jesus asked out loud "What is all this arguing about?"

A man in the crowd spoke up and said, "Teacher, I brought my son for you to heal him. He can't speak because he is possessed by an evil spirit that won't let him talk. And whenever this evil spirit seizes him, it throws him violently to the ground and makes him foam at the mouth and grind his teeth and become rigid. So, I asked your disciples to cast out the evil spirit, but they couldn't do it."

This man was bringing his son to Jesus, but Jesus wasn't there, so the man asked the disciples to cast out the evil spirit, but they couldn't do it. This looked bad for the disciples because they were perceived as having the same powers as Jesus since they walked directly with Jesus. Which is how believers who walk with Jesus should be. This obviously upset Jesus that they couldn't handle the situation and on top of not being able to cast out the evil spirit, the disciples were standing there arguing with other religious law teachers! (Shaking my head).

Jesus said to the disciples, obviously irritated, "You faithless people! How long must I be with you until you believe? How long must I put up with you? Bring the boy to me." Jesus was livid. He said, "How long must I put up with you?!"

They brought the boy to Jesus. And when the demon saw Jesus, it threw the child into a violent convulsion, and he fell to the ground, writhing and foaming at the mouth. In my mind I'm thinking the demon was trying to kill the boy before Jesus could cast him out. The demon wasn't worried about the other disciples because he knew they didn't have the power of faith to cast him out from the boy. But once Jesus walked on the scene, I guess the demon thought he better hurry up and stop tormenting the child slowly and just destroy and kill the child because Jesus was about to set the child free. I wonder what great call and purpose this child had on his life that Satan wanted to destroy the child's mission and ultimately kill the child? I know that child did something great for the Kingdom of Heaven even beyond being in the Bible forever because of the grip the demon had on the boy from such a young age. Satan was trying to kill the child, and it was evident to the boy's father.

Jesus asked the boy's father, "How long has this been happening to the boy?" The father replied, "Since he was very small. The evil spirit often makes him fall into the fire or into water, trying to kill him. Have mercy on us and help us," then this man had the audacity to say to Jesus, "Do something *if you can."*

Oh lawd, what he go and say that for! Jesus is already livid at the lack of power and faith his very own disciples displayed when they couldn't cast out the demon. Now this man blatantly doubting Jesus to His face and had the audacity to say to Jesus, "if you can!"

Jesus was like, "What do you mean, 'if I can'? Anything is possible if a person believes." I can imagine Jesus looking at that man like he had lost his little mind saying some craziness like that to Him. You know Jesus is a thug! Homey don't play that!

That man got some act right real quick and instantly replied, "I do believe, but help me not to doubt!" That was a quick comeback, and it saved him from Jesus going off on him some more. Or maybe it was because the crowd was getting larger from all the commotion and fussing going on that stopped Jesus from addressing the unbelief of the father because Jesus went on and rebuked the evil spirit. But the point is, people do believe, yet they pray in doubt. Jesus can't help you with your doubt, you must help yourself with your doubt by studying the Word to build your faith. Faith comes by hearing, and hearing by the Word of God. Romans 10:17.

You are going to face many evil spirits in your lifetime, and you need to have the power of faith to have the authority to cast them out of your way. And you also need to be able to pray to God for what you want and what you need in faith without a doubt.

Jesus identified the evil spirit and called it by name saying directly to the evil spirit, "Spirit of deafness and muteness, I command you to come out of this child and never enter him again!"

Then the spirit screamed and threw the boy into another violent convulsion before it left him. The boy was laying there motionless, and he appeared to be dead. A murmur ran through the crowd, "He's dead." But Jesus took the boy by the hand and helped him to his feet, and he stood up. Even the crowd was doubting Jesus. Jesus can raise the dead! What's wrong with these people!?

Afterward, when Jesus was alone in the house with his disciples, they asked Him, "Why couldn't we cast out that evil spirit?"

Jesus replied, "This kind can be cast out only by prayer." In other words, whatever they were saying was not prayer. When the disciples tried to cast out the demonic spirit, they had doubt that the spirit would leave the boy. Just saying words to God is not what prayer is. Prayer is a solemn request to God for help, with the assurance that God will answer your call. This story demonstrates to us that if you pray with doubt, it really isn't prayer at all. It's just rambling powerless and useless words. To pray effectively, you must pray with assured faith for your prayers to be heard and *even defined as prayer.*

The second part of the definition of prayer is to give praise and thanks. I believe once we pray knowing our prayers are answered, the praise and thanks we give behind it activates the power propelled by faith.

Philippians 4:6 tells us not to worry about anything at all, but instead pray to God for what you need and give Him thanks. Because God does answer prayer.

22

CHAPTER 22

GOD WILL

We know that God can do anything, but is God willing? In the New Testament is a story of a man with leprosy. Mark 1:40-45.

Leprosy was an incurable disease. Many different skin diseases were classified as leprosy. People with leprosy were outcasted from the community and considered unclean. They couldn't participate in religious services or social activities. People would even throw rocks at them to keep them from coming too close. In other words, a person with leprosy was disgusting to most people. A lot of times people are looked upon as disgusting because they may be homeless, or because of their occupation, or a disease or disability that is beyond their control, even alcoholics or drug addicts are looked upon as disgusting, and as unfortunate as it is many people with mental health issues are also looked down upon. Whatever the reason for being looked upon as disgusting, God is willing to heal that person from any condition.

If the leprosy is incurable, yet God was willing to cure it, then it was incurable by man only. God can and God is willing to heal us from any condition. Curable or incurable by man. But take note that there are many conditions that we face in life that only God can cure.

This leper came to Jesus and kneeled down in front of Jesus and said, "If You are willing, you can make me clean." The leper had no doubt and used complete faith and assurance when he kneeled and prayed to Jesus. Jesus did not throw rocks at the leper or tell the leper not to come close to Him. Our conditions that may be disgusting to man, is not at all disgusting to God. He does not look at us that way at all. Jesus was moved with compassion when the leper came to him in this manner. This is how God looks at us when we come to Him for healing and deliverance of our circumstances.

Jesus said to the leper, "I am willing; be cleansed." Have no doubt, God is willing to answer your prayers.

23

CHAPTER 23

IT'S ALREADY DONE

Mark 11:24 says, "Therefore, I tell you, all the things you pray and ask for, believe that you have received them, and you will have them.

This is a huge key to manifest and create the life you desire. We know God can and we know that God will but know that God has already done! What you are asking God for was already placed inside of you as a desire because it was already determined by God that it is His will for you to have that very thing that you are praying for. Which means that it is already yours and God is just waiting for you to ask Him for it so He can bless you with it! Mark 11:24 solidifies that very concept. Your blessings are waiting on you to seek them out and ask for them in the appropriate season.

God is all knowing. He already knows what you need and want before you ask. Your provision is already made for you before you need it and when you ask for it, it is simply provided by manifesting for you. Perfect faith is a faith that knows it is already done and you can just thank God with that assurance.

This is what makes prayer so powerful, "All things that you pray and ask, believe that you have received them, and you will have them." It's a done deal. What makes prayer powerless is when you pray without the assurance that it is already done; when you pray and still have doubt. That doubt interferes with you receiving what you are asking for.

The other thing that interferes with you receiving what you are asking for is asking for something that is not in God's will for you to have. If it is not already on reserve for you, it's not meant for you to have, therefore you are wasting time and prayer asking for something that is not in God's will for you to have.

The dangerous thing is if you receive what is not in God's will for you to have, it is always a bad outcome for you. The king of darkness hears your prayers as well and can give you what you shouldn't have just to cause you to stumble and fall. your flesh can also go after what you shouldn't, and you will end up in a fallen state because you desired and possessed something that was not in God's will for you to have. You must be very careful with this. It happens to us all at some point in our lives so don't feel bad, just grow and learn so you can avoid things that cause you to stumble.

24

CHAPTER 24

A BATTLE

You know how some people are jealous and don't want to see you succeed, don't want you to have earthly gain, nor do they want you to do well in life? They just want to see you down and secretly want you to fail at all your endeavors. It's like that in the Heavenly realm as well. The demonic forces are against you on Earth and in Heaven. You have angels and spiritual guides that fight for you and on your behalf against the evil spiritual forces that are against you. They fight for you in the Heavenly realm.

Your prayers will activate your very own personal spiritual army to move on your behalf. As soon as you pray for something, demonic forces perk up and begin to try to stop you from receiving the blessing. Some battles are harder and longer than others. Since it is your prayers, thanksgiving, praise, and perseverance that fuel your personal spiritual warriors, you must continue to pray for that which you are believing God for until it manifests. Luke 18:1 says, "They ought always to pray and not lose heart." 1Thessalonians 5:16 says, "Pray without ceasing." This is because it is how the battle is won. Praying is a part of the full armor of God mentioned in Ephesians 6 because it is a powerful tool in spiritual warfare. Pray in perfect faith, and don't stop until you receive. That's when the battle is won.

Praying for others also activates your blessings into manifestation. It helps them fight for the blessing that they need and in return we will receive back what we are giving out. Others will pray for you in your time of need for your blessing to manifest. The more warriors the better, especially the greater the battle.

Being envious and jealous of others blocks your blessings. You get in your own way by harboring jealousy. Withholding knowledge from others is a form of jealousy and blocks your blessings and can actually cause you to lose the blessings you currently have. God gives but it can be taken away as well. Do what is right so that your blessings come and remain.

25

CHAPTER 25

RELATIONSHIP WISDOM

Loving Yourself

After your relationship with God, the next important relationship is your relationship with yourself. You know who God is, you know that God loves you, and you know that you love God, is my presumption. But do you love yourself?

Before you can have a healthy functioning relationship with a mate, you need to know who you are, be comfortable with who you are, and love who you are.

As simple as this may seem, so many of us don't know who we are and don't love who we are. Everyone is not comfortable in their skin and rejects who they truly are because they don't love themselves.

I believe many people do not love themselves because they were not properly loved as children. As parents we are to protect our children from all harm. This includes providing a safe environment for them to learn and grow with the supervision, love, and care of their parents. As parents we are to feed, clothe, educate, and provide medical care for our children.

Unfortunately, we have stories of sexual abuse, physical abuse, emotional abuse, and neglect all stemming from mistreatment during our childhood. As a result, we don't know how to love others, and we do not love ourselves.

The Bible clearly tells parents not to anger or exasperate their children. Any type of abuse during adulthood leaves us angry as adults, imagine the lifelong damage it can cause when done to children whose brains are still trying to process life and develop.

A child's mind is not capable of handling trauma the way an adult may handle the same traumatic situation. Abusing children stunts the normal mental development of the child. The child cannot comprehend that the abusive act against them was not their fault. As a child, the child will blame themselves for being abused and begin to feel inadequate and inferior towards their own selves. The child will continue to grow into adulthood with the same damaging perception of themselves. Thus, rendering them incapable of properly loving themselves and others.

As adults, many people wonder why they seem to not be able to have a healthy relationship with a mate, not realizing it may stem from their troubled childhood. It takes years to fix and recover from trauma that happened in a matter of seconds. Imagine if the trauma was continual as a child, such as sexual abuse, and how much damage it does and how long it will take during adulthood to correct. That's only if the person decides to receive counseling, medication if needed, and self-help practices to heal from the damage done to them during childhood. Few people take this step towards healing from childhood abuse, and the world ends up with damaged adults damaging other adults in relationships. The environment also ends up with adults forming addictions to cope with childhood trauma.

Fredrick Douglas put it this way, "It is easier to build strong children than to repair broken adults." As parents, we must do our best to protect our children from any abuse, neglect, or harm. It's imperative for them to love themselves and to be able to grow up knowing how to love others, and necessary for them to have healthy loving relationships.

To do this, a person must know how to love oneself first before they can train a child to do the same. Do you see the broken cycle here? Being that you lead by example for your children, and if you are a poor example for them, then your children will adopt your inadequate patterns as they grow and take this into their own adult lives. Again, producing dysfunctional relationships.

You must start with yourself. You must be determined to heal and to love yourself with the same 1Corithians Chapter 13 love that the Bible instructs us to have. Often times people can be so hard on themselves, but loving yourself means forgiving yourself, being patient and kind to yourself, and show yourself all the attributes given in the Bible as an example of Godly love. You must apply these to yourself and master this concept of loving. Then you can effectively love others with the same Godly love as commanded to do. (Love thy neighbor).

If you know that you have not healed from your past, it is very important that you seek out your healing process with a professional as soon as possible because if you do not, it will hinder your progress towards fulfilling your purpose in life. The pain of not dealing with your traumatic childhood will manifest itself in your relationships with significant others. When this happens, you are unable to continue towards your destiny, because of the hinderance of tumultuous relationships not allowing you to focus on anything else but the dysfunctional relationship.

Peculiar People

God's chosen people are a peculiar type of people. Other non-Godly people find peculiar people strange. God's Chosen people are merely different because they are not doing what worldly people do. They do not process thought the same way worldly people do. Instead, God's Chosen people are doing what God says for them to do and have programmed their minds to think and feel as instructed in the Bible. This is strange to those who don't understand this way of life, because people who do not acknowledge God as the head of their lives in the way that they live their lives, think selfishly, and do what they want and choose to do instead of seeking out God's will for their lives and doing that instead. They acknowledge God from their mouths but their choice to do as they please clearly show the lack of reverence for God in their lives.

As a result, those who are led by the Holy Spirit are targeted and ridiculed, slandered, set up for failure, outcasted, betrayed, and rejected. I have come to tell you that this is the intentional work of the enemy to keep the Chosen from pursuing their Divine Purpose.

The enemy comes to steal, destroy, and kill. I swap the order from the way it is stated in the Bible because I feel the enemy's attack is often to steal from us what is necessary to carry out our Divine mission. Then he tries to destroy our purpose and us along with it, and ultimately kill our purpose and eventually kill us too. The job of Satan is ultimately to take life. Our spiritual life, and then our physical life. Often times Satan does this by using a significant other or mate.

Many people have given up their dreams and goals because the relationship they have entered into is preventing them from moving forward with their destiny. They sit stagnant because instead of them realizing what has taken place, they feel it wasn't for them to fulfill that particular destiny. But the truth of the matter is, God placed that dream in their hearts for them to recognize why He created them and to pursue that very thing that they have now cast to the side because of the dysfunctionality of their present relationship.

God's Chosen People

God's chosen people are a light in this world. There are guidelines given to the chosen on how they should live their life here on Earth. Living your life this way is a key part in the equation of living a successful and prosperous life. This includes shining your light in the darkness to draw others into the light and into living this very same way of life. Light draws people in and people follow light. Light brightens up a darkened space. Being a light requires having relationships of all kinds. Having a "right" relationship requires discipline and a certain way of living.

Ephesians 5:1-20

"Follow God's example in everything you do because you are His dear children. Live a life filled with love for others, following the example of Christ, who loved you and gave Himself as a sacrifice to take away your sins. And God was pleased because that sacrifice was like sweet perfume to him.

Let there be no sexual immorality, impurity, or greed amongst you. Such sins have no place among God's people. Obscene stories, foolish talk, and coarse jokes, these are not for you. Instead let there be thankfulness to God. You can be sure that no immoral, and pure, or greedy person will inherit the Kingdom of Christ. For a greedy person is really an idolator who worships the things of this world. Don't be fooled by those who try to excuse these sins, but the terrible anger of God comes upon all those who disobey him. Don't participate in the things these people do. For though your hearts were once full of darkness, now you are full of light from the Lord, and your behavior should show it! For this light within you produces only what is good and right and true.

Try to find out what is pleasing to the Lord. Take no part in the worthless deeds of evil and darkness, instead, rebuke and expose them. It is shameful even to talk about the things that ungodly people do in secret. But when the light shines on them, it becomes clear how evil those things are. And where your light shines, it will expose their evil deeds. This is why it is said, "**awake, O sleeper, rise from the dead, and Christ will give you light**".

So be careful how you live, not as fools but as those who are wise. Make the most of every opportunity for doing good in these evil days. Don't act thoughtlessly but try to understand what the Lord wants you to do. Don't be drunk with alcohol because that will ruin your life. Instead, let the Holy Spirit fill and control you. Then you will sing psalms and hymns and spiritual songs amongst yourselves, making music to the Lord in your hearts. And you will always give thanks for everything to God the father in the name of our Lord Jesus Christ."

This is one of the references in the Bible that tells us how to live our life on Earth as the light of this world and to expose evil.

There are currently some "woke" Chosen few who are boldly speaking out about what is "right" and what is "wrong" in our society today. Those who are opposed are trying to shut them up. They slander their names and even try to find reason to put them in jail and mental hospitals and drug them with manmade medicines to alter and control their minds. To shut them up and to hide the light of the truth to a lost and dark world.

There are things that take place that are very evil and demonic, and few people are even aware that they are happening. Amongst the elite of this world, so much evilness is running rampant, and the average Joe and Jane Blow are unaware and live their lives unaware. However, God has a few Chosen that were created to expose and fight against these evils. Pray for them always.

26

CHAPTER 26

MENTAL DISORDERS

Mental illness is not new, and the Bible gives us stories of God's people who suffered from and what would be classified today as mental disorders. Many Christians and spiritual people have what this society would call mental illness. It may not be talked about because it is seen as a demonic condition just like the leper in the Bible. God can heal any condition or illness, make no mistake about that.

Paul in the Bible talked about a thorn in his side that he begged God over and over to remove. We don't know what that "thorn" was, but we do know there is no perfect person. I'm sure Paul had that thorn for a reason. I have several thorns. Lol. And I admit that my "thorns" keep me leaning on the Lord and in prayer.

A lot of my thorns have been diagnosed to be symptoms of Post-Traumatic Stress Disorder, because of traumatic events that took place in my life. A lot of the symptoms I have that the doctor calls PTSD are the exact things that keep me on my knees and in direct relationship with my Creator.

I refuse to allow anyone else to define who I am. I know who I am. I am aware that many people, even some of my own loved ones, do not understand me. People belittle, misjudge, tear down, and ostracize who and what they don't understand, and I am not trying to explain myself or reason with anyone who refuses to understand. Instead of focusing on their own shortcomings, people will allow the enemy to use them to slander and hurt others, especially a child of God.

That child of God needs to understand this is a trick of the enemy to get them off course. The weight of your purpose can get you down and it will come with periods of bouts that can fall under the category of mental illness. You are different. You will be blatantly attacked by the enemy even as a child, to try to stop you from accomplishing what you were created to do, and the unfortunate characteristic result may be classified under a mental illness.

I am speaking to God's Chosen. Not someone who is possessed with a demonic spirit that causes them to have strong symptoms of mental illness. There is a clear difference. This Chosen person of God who gets down with the weight of their calling, who is paranoid of people and don't trust easily because of the ridicule and horrible treatment they have endured because of whose they are. This person I am speaking to needs to know you are not alone. You can have a mental diagnosis and be a complete true soldier for Christ and achieve true success and wealth. You are normal in your own right; you just think differently from how the world wants you to think.

The whole idea of faith is the definition of a mental illness. Believing in something you cannot see, or feel is not looked at as sane. Talking to a Spiritual Deity and hearing the same Deity speak to you, is classified as insane. Because no one is physically there.

Be very aware of who you are and whose you are. Be very aware of how you think, respond, and feel. Don't let labels define who you are, know who you are. Always seek to grow, learn, and heal in your awareness.

Just like Paul begged God to remove his thorn over and over, many mental disorders cannot be "prayed or fasted away". Even when others don't understand you and your mental disorder, you need to know you are not alone and there are doctors to help you just like there are doctors to help cancer patients, diabetic patients, etc. It is not a test of your faith nor is it punishment from God.

Demonic attacks will bring trauma to you and cause you to move and feel differently. Humans label it as a mental disorder and sometimes the trauma may cause a chemical imbalance within your brain waves. If you read the stories of Job, Jeremiah, David, Elijah, John the Baptist, and Paul, just to name a few, you will see many symptoms of what we label as Mental Disorders. We as Christians will suffer, and the Word of God tells us that. But in reading the stories of these few biblical characters pay attention to their success despite what modern day medicine now classifies as mental disorders. Be encouraged by that. You are not alone, and it is much more common and prevalent than the world is allowing us to know. On purpose.

It would be wonderful if the "church" would be open and honest about the stress, struggles, and traumas of life and how living in this world has affected and changed them mentally. But instead, the church chooses to wear a mask, and this is living a lie within the Christian community. I encourage you to change this and bring forth awareness of how you love the Lord, and how you are walking in your Divine purpose with what the world calls Bi-Polar disorder, schizophrenia disorder, post-traumatic stress disorder, depression, and any disorder that falls under mental illness. And you are successful in all that you do despite the attempts of the enemy to destroy your mind. It's just a necessary thorn that turns into a testimony!

27

CHAPTER 27

LIVING IN SINGLETOWN

This chapter will address mostly single people but everyone, single or not, needs to read it.

Sliding In My DM

Him: not tooting a horn or anything but I can satisfy you Sugar if you up for it and if I had a chance. Sugar: I told you before I'm not looking for a relationship

Him: that word relationship. One day in the future we should discuss the word.

Sugar: what is there to discuss?

Him: It is just a word. There are scumbag men who know y'all women like the word and use it for their benefit.

Sugar: commitment. monogamous. exclusive.

Him: nobody has to prove anything to women anymore, so the only men who are losing out of finding healthy discourse with women are men who tell the truth. Liars are the only ones winning which is why we have so many podcasts about relationships and heartbreak because men who lie keep getting a chance.

Sugar: commitment. monogamous. exclusive.

Him: you really repeated the same thing. lol.

Sugar: because you didn't acknowledge it.

Him: I understand as an intelligent woman that's what it means to you, Sugar. But men will just say they want it to just reap the benefits, then it's too late once you realize it.

Sugar: I know, that's the purpose of seeking out someone that is honest. And seeking out someone that is not trying to have sex right up front and is willing to wait because they really want the relationship. I have sex if I want to have sex. Without the expectation of anything more. If I want to and right now, I don't want to. I may just want to wait until after I marry before having sex.

Him: I understand. I just have to hope to be around when you change your mind and want to.

Sugar: it won't happen. You shouldn't want that.

Helm: why shouldn't I?

Sugar: you should want a good woman for yourself.

Him: why though? It's no difference. People have good women for themselves and still don't have a Peace of Mind or it still don't work out. The Lord has truly blessed me, I have a great job, family, I am healthy, own my home. I just want someone to cuddle with from time to time but I don't want someone of my own. I don't want that responsibility.

Sugar: whyyyyyyyyyyyy

him: what I realized from these liars and cheaters is that they need women. That's why they prey on them. since I don't need a woman to prey on, I look at life differently.

Sugar: some people actually want a life partner.

Him: I want companionship but don't want to have someone in my face 24/7.

Sugar: if you work it's not 24/7.

Him: the divorce rate shows they don't want a relationship. Look how many of us are single. And I'm a part of the few men who are single for a certain reason. Everybody else is single because of manipulation or lies or cheating.

Sugar: they should stay and work the marriage out.

Him: like if you were going to cheat why be in a relationship?

Sugar: not get out the marriage. People make mistakes.

Him: Why humiliate the person you love?

Sugar: so basically, you are afraid of being hurt?

Him: I'm not afraid of being hurt. I'm not giving up my peace. I treat people well. And will continue to. I just know I don't want the responsibility of having someone solely of my own. Sometimes I don't want to be bothered, and you can't do that in a relationship. Sometimes I want to travel alone and do what I want without having to worry about hurting someone.

Sugar: people need to work their relationships out. And not be afraid of being married to the same person for a lifetime.

Him: maybe it's the men who don't want to work it out. Maybe they want to be free. I believe women will work it out. I truly believe most divorces are the men fault. I think they don't want to go to counseling or work it out because they can't be free to do what they want. Men are just selfish. My mom and her friends say these older men be married and still hit on women. Like you not happy fam? You ready to spend money on another woman when you can be spending that money on your wife? Your family? The energy these dudes put into cheating could easily be put into their relationship. Instead of buying a random woman you don't know a drink at the bar. Take your wife out and buy her a drink. Text your wife she's beautiful instead of these Instagram women who attention you trying to get.

Sugar: if you know that, then be that man.

Him: for what? I have to first get married. I am that man. I'm honest, like the rest of these men should be.

Sugar: Okay honey.

Him: Why didn't you stay with your husband Sugar? You tried to work it out? Most likely you did. He was the one who didn't try, I bet.

Sugar: Your right.

Him: It never fails. The hardest thing to do is to tell a woman what's on your mind and give her the chance to decide. Men scared to lose that way. So, they say what they know women want to hear, smh. You got to give people a chance though Sugar.

Sugar: What do you mean?

Him: When I say people, I mean me. Like whenever you need company.

Sugar: Lol.

Him: You never know. You might enjoy my company.

Sugar: As long as sex is not involved.

Him: Lol. No sex? I'm too old for that.

Sugar: Lol.

Him: I'm 37 Sugar.

Sugar: And?

Him: I'm too old to be just hanging with a female I'm sexually attracted to like a gay best friend, while another man gets to reap the benefits, cause eventually you will get the urge. And somebody else will get the privilege. But I tried. You can't say I didn't show interest. On multiple occasions.

Two Days Later @ 1am

Him: Sugar?

Sugar: why are you up?

Him: thinking about you.

Sugar: I've been having trouble sleeping and you woke me.

Him: Maybe I can help you sleep. I told you that you got to give people a chance Sugar.

Sugar: let me explain to you what the problem is with the way that you're thinking. Women are receivers. They receive what you pour into them mentally, spiritually, physically, and sexually. When you are having sex with a woman you are depositing into her what is inside of you. There is a spiritual deposit that is taking place and there's also a natural deposit that is taking place. This causes a bond within her. This causes her to desire you more. This causes her to become what you are in part. And that what you have deposited into her yearns for you more and more. We call this, developing feelings or a bond. So now this woman has feelings for you, all of these emotions are going on inside of her because she wants more of you then you want to give to her naturally. Because you're not understanding that you are depositing yourself deep within her, and that is causing her to want even more of you. That's causing her to have parts of you within her and she begins to feel as though she is deeply in love with you. So, you can't just have a sexual relationship with a female and expect her not to have feelings for you. There's no way around it. And this is how the woman ends up getting hurt. This is how domestic violence gets started when there's a chick on the side. The sad thing is, for some reason women don't understand their own self, they don't understand this process. And the men don't care because it isn't them getting hurt. They don't have a conscious, they don't feel bad, until something drastic takes place. There's no way in hell that I want to continue to do things like this to myself. It's a type of suicide. Something within me dies every time I put myself in a situation like this outside of marriage, because outside of marriage it is my own fault because I knew better. Inside the marriage it is the husband's fault because he is responsible for the well-being of his wife naturally, spiritually, mentally, and physically.

Him: wow. I see your points. I learned something new. How was your day? When can I get the phone number?

Sugar: SMH!

Word To the Women

I have found that men make a decision to love. Women fall into what they think is love just by spending time or having a sexual relationship with a man. And then she wonders why that man does not feel the same way about her or how he can end up in a committed relationship with a different female, and she was having sex with him regularly the entire time and the man never fell in love with her or gave her a commitment.

This is because men are wired in a way that they will not fall in love unless they make the decision to do so. When they decide that they want to be in a committed relationship with a female and have love for or fall in love with a particular female, it is then and only then, that they will express feelings of love and commitment. It doesn't matter how good you are to him, it doesn't matter how much you give to him of yourself or your services, it doesn't even matter to him if you express having feelings of love for him, nothing that you do will make a man love you unless he decides to.

Men will continue to have sex with you and other women at the same time, and suddenly decide they want to commit to or wife a certain female and cut you and all others off that they were dealing with sexually. Save yourself the trouble and do not give so much to this man and do not expect to get in return what you are giving to him, unless he expresses to you that he wants a committed relationship with you. It is not until then that you will get a commitment from him, and you will only be doing yourself emotional harm.

Pursuing a man without a commitment from him is not a good thing at all to go through because focusing on your goals and purpose will be difficult to do at this point. If you conduct yourself in this manner with a man, your goals and purpose may even be pushed to the back burner while dealing with the unpleasant emotions this type of behavior will bring. Rejection being the main hurtful emotion you will experience.

Community Sexing

I have met a lot of single men who have full or joint custody of their children. Most of them want to remain single. They throw themselves into their occupation and into raising their children. They also entertain a variety of women sexually and do not allow a closeness to develop between them and any of these females they are sexually involved with. This behavior most likely comes from the pain of a failed marriage or relationship. This sexual behavior comes from relationship insecurity due to lack of trust in a mate but satisfying the need for sexual release with the help of a partner.

The single females I have met can be all over the place. Some cut off having a relationship or dating completely, others entertain several men sexually, and then others fall into a depression and remain bitter after failed marriages or failed relationships.

In either case, these behaviors are unhealthy behaviors and counseling and/or divorce care classes should have been a part of the healing process.

One of the dangers of this type of behavior outside of the individual is the impact that it has on their children. The children learn how to have a relationship from the example of the parent.

Please know that even if you try to hide the multiple sex partners you have from your children, they will know if not now, eventually. What's done in the dark always comes to light. You are teaching your children that once a relationship has issues it's best to walk away from that person or your marriage instead of hanging in there and working things out. Then you send the message to them that it is okay to be promiscuous and have multiple sex partners.

This is how we have children who have different mothers or different fathers. This is not what God planned for us. And it is not at all a healthy way to live, and it does not set a good example for our children to follow. In fact, it's most likely setting our children up to also have failed relationships and repeat this pattern of multiple sex partners because it is what they saw their parent do who they admire and love greatly.

As for the men, daughters look up to their fathers to show them how they should be treated by a male figure in a relationship. This shows them they can be mistreated and used as a piece of property that is not worthy of love from who they are sexing. Boys look to their fathers to show them how to be a man. This type of behavior is teaching the boy to devalue the woman and have several sexual partners void of closeness and intimacy. We should all want our children to find love in a lasting, healthy, loving marriage. But if that's not the example set for them, then how can anyone expect them to find such?

Even if we grew up as children in an unhealthy environment, without a parent, or poor examples of how a healthy relationship should look, we need to be wise and mature enough to heal and learn how to enjoy a healthy relationship, how to work through the ups and downs of relationships and stay together. We need to start showing our youth how to have a healthy family dynamic to build stronger families. Society complains about the mindset of the youth but ignores that this mindset most likely comes from what they have learned in their own family origin growing up. Somewhere a change needs to take place, and that change starts with you and your behaviors within your household.

You must show your children what a healthy, loving, marriage looks like by actually having one.

This is particularly so for the men. I believe men do not understand the level of their influence and how heavily their decisions affect their children. Even a father who is absent in his child's life, speaks volumes to that child through his absence. The father that is present has an even greater effect on his child than that!

Our children are growing up in abnormal family dynamics, witnessing their parents have unhealthy relationships, multiple sex partners, and to our children this behavior seems to be healthy and/or normal because it's all they know. Do you see the monster we are creating here?

Men, the Bible tells us a man who finds a wife finds a good thing, and he obtains favor from the Lord. Do you know you hold up your blessings because you want to be single and have multiple sex partners? You think you are good, right? But you are wrong, you are not experiencing the fullness in life that God has for you. You are void of favor. You cannot obtain the blessings God has for you without God's favor upon your life.

The Bible doesn't say this about the woman, only the man. This is important for the man to grasp when it comes to wealth building, because you can accomplish so much more with the right woman as your wife in a healthy marriage, and your children and children's children will be blessed from the favor God has bestowed upon you. When you mess up this pattern you destroy your family for generations to come. Creating generational curses upon your very own children which are passed down to their children. It is crucial in the family dynamic that the man lead his children by example and make wise, healthy decisions with relationships and intimacy. Community sexing is not the correct answer.

Heal and learn to have a healthy marriage that withstands the test of time. Let go of the community sexing and be a husband to a deserving wife and obtain all that God has for you.

Word To the Men

Women are not wired like you. Even if a woman tells you that she can have sex with you and not develop feelings for you, that is not something that a woman is typically wired to do. It's not good to play with another person's feelings. And the reason why I say it's not a wise decision to engage in this type of sexual activity is because you reap what you sow. **The pain that you cause another person is going to come back to you.** That's the law of the universe. Karma is real. Karma is merely a word that simply means you will reap what you sow. Do not take the feelings of any female lightly. If you are going to have a sexual relationship with a female, she is going to develop feelings of love for you. If you do not plan to date her with the intention of marrying her, refrain from sex with her. Fornication causes so many problems when you do it, which is why it's just best that you do not step into these types of relationships. The woman is going to want you to reciprocate what she feels for you. And you're not going to want to reciprocate it if you are only using her for sexual pleasure. It's not a good idea to continue in these types of relationships because it does hinder your blessings.

Do not believe the lie that the devil is putting out in the world, that says marriages will likely fail. Do not believe the lie that every man who is married, is unhappily married so it's better just to stay single or a bachelor and play the field. That is a lie from the pit of hell. You receive more blessings when you find a Good Wife. When you accept and marry a woman you immediately begin to get blessed by God. And that woman will also help you reach greater heights than you could ever imagine reaching alone. If this is the woman that God has sent to you, your success after you marry her will be huge. The peace, the love, the respect, and just being the head and the king of your household will give you a confidence that you can never have as a single man. It is unfortunate that successful marriages do not get publicity like they should. People always focus on the negative. There are plenty of marriages that last a lifetime and withstand the test of every trial and overcome every obstacle that Satan throws their way. These men are happy with their wives, and they understand that no other woman could compare to the wife that God has given them. And although they are tempted, they remain faithful. The devil doesn't want you to see this type of successful lifelong relationship. Do not focus on the negative when it comes to marriage, know that the positive aspect of marriage is far greater than the negative. We need our families to stay together, that is how we build, maintain, and retain the wealth we have built. And it starts with the man accepting his bride and it endures with that man leading as a man of God should.

The marriages that fail, fail because God and Godly principals were not the focus and priority.

The Side Piece and Situationships

The truth of the matter is, there is no gratification in being the side piece of a married individual. On the very surface the time you can spend is limited. Everything you can get, if anything, comes with limitations. The biggest obstacle of all is that you have no rights, and you are not first in that person's life. Why do that to yourself?

Being in this type of relationship is not loving and valuing yourself at all and it comes with consequences that are natural as well as spiritual. It naturally does not feel good to know someone you love and want is sleeping with someone else. You run the risk of diseases as well as domestic conflict and violence can result from these types of encounters. Children can be born out of wedlock and deprived because one parent is married or with someone else. It is a relationship that is filled with lies and decent. The emotional scarring can have a lifelong negative effect on all involved. Being an individual that settles for this type of lifestyle is not showing love for oneself. It's dysfunctional and unhealthy behavior to accept your placement as a side piece or situations that are similar.

There are certain things that we should not do, that are spelled out in the Word of God. The reason we should not do such things is because of the hurt and damage it can cause to those involved and even their generations to come. Lying and Adultery are two of those things.

In any kind of relationship lying affects how a person will think about you from that point on. Your credibility is lost. No one can believe a liar. Relationships are broken because of lies and deceit. When trust is broken it is a hurtful situation. It is easy to lose trust from lies but hard to gain it back if you still want a good relationship with the person that has been lied to. The person that is lying and being deceitful in the relationship has no respect for the current relationship or the individual that they are lying to. Respect is also something that is hard to gain back once you have lied to the individual. If the person you are romantically involved with lies to you on a continual basis, please know and understand that they do not respect your union or you. Respect yourself enough to not remain entangled in a situation that is filled with lies.

Sleeping with a married individual is Adultery. This is wrong to do even if the other partner is aware of your existence. Someone in the union is getting the short end of the stick and it's usually the side piece. The person who has the papers has the rights. Not just on the natural surface but in the spiritual realm. The two that are married are bonded spiritually. The side piece does not have this spiritual bond at all. Spiritually the marriage union is granted certain blessings, and the prayers of one spouse for the other are reverenced and honored. Not so when you are the side piece because you have no spiritual union because there is no marriage. The side piece is much like a prosthetic limb that the other married individual can pick up and put on when they feel like it, and take it off, and put it down when they are finished with it. The person they are married to **is** the attached limb, the rib in fact, that remains and cannot be put on and off no matter how hard they try. Because it is a sin to take part in the act of Adultery, your prayers will hit the ceiling and fall to the ground. If you remain in that sinful situation, you will also remain out of the will of God. You will not be spiritually blessed until you get out of it. Even if it looks and feels good for a moment, the good feeling will come to an end in its time.

Value yourself enough to get out of these types of situations. You cannot grow, you cannot advance because you need the aid of the Holy Spirit to do so. This type of situation consumes the side piece, and they cannot focus on just themselves. Therefore, it will benefit you to remove yourself from such a situation if this is what you are entertaining. You want to prosper in life, not hinder it.

In the biblical story of Sarah, Abraham, and Hagar, we see that Sarah and Abraham are married. Sarah could not conceive a child for Abraham at that moment. Why? Because it is not yet her time to do so. Remember everything has its time and place. Hagar is a servant to Sarah. Sarah allowed Abraham to have sex with Hagar so that she would conceive a child for Abraham. Once Hagar did conceive the child for Abraham it caused a lot of tension between Sarah and Hagar which ended up in Sarah demanding that Abraham send Hagar away. Which he did, Abraham sent Hagar and her child away homeless.

If we apply this story to the current situation of the side piece. Then Hagar would be the side piece. Hagar is a servant remember? Which explains the duty of any side piece, which is to do nothing but serve another woman's husband's need for intimacy and to provide for him what the wife is not giving him at the moment. Eventually, this will cause strife and tension within the trio and the side piece will be expelled and left hurting. The man is not going to leave his rib, and he will quickly get rid of the side piece and any children that she may have had with him, with little care to how they will survive in this world.

Do not put yourself in such a situation and if you are in it, do not remain. The moment you leave and begin your healing journey you will grow and be able to focus on you and your aspirations. (This situation is also in reverse, and men can be side pieces too!)

Red Flags

A person cannot get back what they cannot give. In order to give and receive something you must have an understanding of it and be familiar with it.

If someone doesn't know how to love, they cannot receive the love you give to them. They have no understanding of it. They cannot properly receive what they do not understand because they are not able to process it internally. It's a waste of your time and effort to expect to get something from someone that they don't have to give. And if they do not know how to give love, nor have the proper understanding of it, they are also incapable of receiving it from you.

There are behaviors that people display that let you know they cannot give or receive love in a healthy manner. These are called red flags.

It's a fine line between the red flags and giving someone a chance. Be careful with giving them the benefit of doubt or giving them the opportunity to change questionable behavior. You must carry everything to God in prayer.

I know you think that He may not answer but God really does, and He will show you if the behavior is a red flag or if it's a changeable behavior.

"What a friend we have in Jesus, all our sins and griefs to bear. Oh, what a privilege to carry everything to God in prayer. Oh, what peace we often forfeit, oh what needless pain we bear. All because we do not carry, everything to God in prayer." These lyrics are true wisdom and Godly advice.

An individual must want to change for change to take place. They must first admit that there is a problem with the current behavior and then accept that a change is needed. Only then can a behavior change in an individual. Even with that, it will take time, patience, and determination for the change to take place and be an effective change of that behavior.

One of the mistakes often made in the beginning of relationships is ignoring the red flags. It is important to look out for and note red flags. These are behaviors of people that should be avoided. There are many red flags, and some can be tailored for just you that may not be a problem for someone else. What doesn't work for you, do not make excuses for, and move on to another prospect.

Here is a list of 10 red flags that I feel should be a deal breaker and 3 bonus things to look out for:

1. Abusive behavior. Which means the intentional use of physical, sexual, verbal, or emotional abuse against a peer or dating partner. This includes physically hitting or striking, forcing sexual acts, name calling, humiliating, controlling, intimidation, manipulation, being secretive and evasive, harassment, angers easily, coercion, gaslighting, isolating you from your family and friends, threatening, yelling, ignoring your attempts to communicate or the silent treatment, checking out other people openly in your presence, and cursing at you.
2. Substance Addictions. Once you notice the overuse of alcohol or any drug, run.
3. Excessive lying. Some people just lie when it's no reason to even lie. They make up stories just to be talking and painting a false picture for no significant reason. Then there are those that lie because they have wrong

intentions for you. Whatever the reason for the lies, it is a behavior that is against the commandment of God, nature, and now you. Avoid dealing with this person.

4. Not responding to calls and texts in a timely manner. This is a sign that you are not a priority in this individual's life. If they are claiming to be so busy with family or work that they cannot respond in a timely manner to your calls or text, they are not ready for a relationship or not interested in you being a priority in their life.

5. Not spending time with you. If the person is always too busy with family or work or too tired from work or their children to spend time or make time for you, they are not worth the trouble and have no genuine interest in you.

6. Rushing the relationship. Also known as "Love bombing". If they don't want to take the time allotted to get to know you at an agreed upon pace, this is a huge red flag. You should be comfortable with the pace of the relationship and not feel rushed in the progression.

7. Lack of Communication. Communication is a key element to any relationship. If it is lacking the relationship will not be healthy. A person that is emotionally unavailable and refuses to communicate and express their feelings should be avoided.

8. Unwillingness to compromise. This type of person is selfish, stubborn, and self-centered. This type of behavior will cause you to feel as though you are giving way more than you are receiving. A recipe for a disastrous relationship.

9. Inconsistency. The person of interest should be just as interested in you. You should not feel as though you are "working" for their attention or your place in their life. If you are unaware of where the relationship stands and not sure of what is going on with your partner this is a red flag. Forming a connection with the other person takes consistency from both individuals.

10. Breadcrumbing. This is when the person is giving you bits and pieces of encouragement for a relationship to sustain. They give just enough so you don't give up on the relationship. When you move towards

them, they move away. If you withdraw your efforts, they increase their advances towards you. This is a noncommittal individual.

11. If you must chase them, they are not for you.

12. If they can't accept your past, they are not for you. Your mate will be able to accept your past and maturely allow you room to make the necessary changes that need to be made for a successful relationship without holding your past against you.

13. If they do not acknowledge their mistakes and grow from them, they will not make a good mate.

If you are unhappy more often than you are happy in a relationship, that is not a good sign. You should explore why you are unhappy and reconsider remaining in the relationship if there are no positive changes. How you feel about a person is different from how they make you feel. How they make you feel is the true reality of the relationship.

Ignoring these red flags will prevent you from being able to effectively work towards and achieve your goals and aspirations. Avoid falling into this trap.

28

CHAPTER 28

NO ONE'S DREAM IS MORE IMPORTANT THAN YOUR OWN

Be careful not to give a person too much of yourself and/or your time. This is something you cannot do in any relationship because you run the risk of making them and their goals more important than your own if you do so. Nothing or no one is more important than what you were created to do. Not your spouse, not your parents, not your children. Their dreams, goals, and aspirations are not more important than your own. Allow them the space to achieve their goals and work towards them without you sacrificing too much of yourself.

In any relationship you must be able to still accomplish your dreams and goals. When in a marriage you should support and be supportive of one another's goals. No one's goals or dreams should be put off for the other spouse to accomplish theirs instead. Both should be able to pursue their goals simultaneously.

I remember when I was homeschooling my children and dedicating my entire life to my family. I put off writing books and scripts, which was always my dreams and goals to accomplish. One day I talked with a lady on the phone that I didn't really know. It's strange but I don't remember who she was or why we spoke, but I do remember she asked me why I wasn't writing, and I told her I wanted to concentrate on raising my family and I would write once my children were older. She told me she did the same thing with her daughters. She worked three jobs to put her daughters in private school and the extra curriculum activities they wanted to pursue. Once they got older, she said they forgot about her sacrifices for them and didn't appreciate her or show her respect. Her advice to me was to work on my goals and aspirations because when my children become adults they may not appreciate or even remember the sacrifices I made for them. I never met that lady in person or spoke to her again. I do believe the entire purpose for us having that conversation was for her to give me that advice because I have no memory of why we connected and spoke on the phone. I don't know her name, or where she lives.

With regret I say to you, I did not listen to the lady's advice. I thought her advice was ill given and it wouldn't happen to me. How wrong I was! I should have listened to wisdom when she spoke to me on that matter. I am sharing this story with you, the reader, and asking that you not disregard this advice.

I have looked at successful young people who have marriages and families. They are walking in their calling and still maintaining their family. God is giving them the means and Grace to be able to do both. Make sure you do not give too much of yourself and your time to someone else, no matter who they are, and as a result your dreams get lost or pushed to the side even if it is for only a short moment. Your time is for you. Time is something you can't get back. Have the faith and the courage to walk in your purpose and accomplish all that you are called to accomplish right when you know what it is. No matter what, and God will open every door that needs to be opened for you.

29

CHAPTER 29

VOWED IN MARRIAGE

The Commitment

When you take your vows during the marriage ceremony the vows are to God not to the individual. You vow to God that you will remain committed to the individual in different circumstances until death is the dividing factor. Yet the divorce rate is at an all-time high and healing from the trauma of grieving a divorce is as common as the common cold sore. So many people have PTSD from the trauma of divorce, and it goes untreated because they don't seek out professional help and treatment to help during the healing process.

Divorce

Yep...off the rip, I'm going to talk to you about divorce. Divorce is making a promise and then breaking your promise in a way that is very hurtful to all parties involved. There are some cases where divorce is necessary, but in many cases it is not. In most of these cases it is a cowardly and selfish act.

Malachi 2:16 lets us know that God said he hates divorce. Marriage is a lifetime commitment and a relationship that no man should sever.

"Here is another thing you do. You cover the Lord's altar with tears, weeping and groaning because he pays no attention to your offerings, and he doesn't accept them with pleasure. You cry out, why has the Lord abandoned us? I'll tell you why! Because the Lord witnessed the vows you and your wife made to each other on your wedding day when you were young. But you have been disloyal to her, though she remained your faithful companion, the wife of your marriage vows. Didn't the Lord make you one with your wife? In body and spirit, you are his. And what does he want? Godly children from your union. So, guard yourself; Remain loyal to the wife of your youth. For I hate divorce! Says the lord, the God of Israel. It is as cruel as putting on a victim's blood-stained coat, says the Lord almighty so guard yourself; Always remain loyal to your wife." Malachi 2:13-16.

Seems like to me the men folk were thinking the grass was greener on the other side with the side chick, and they started treating their wives bad and abusing them. (Even if it is just lying and neglecting, that is abusive.) Making it seem like something was wrong with the wife to give them a reason to divorce the wife and get with another chick. The side chick was probably in their ear telling them how awful the wife was and how they should divorce her and get with them instead. Because that's how Satan operates.

Now divorced, they get with the side chick and wished they had stayed with their wife. They realized over time that life just got harder because God wasn't hearing their prayers and didn't care about their tears with the new chick because God hates divorce, and they are now divorced from their first wife. God was there as they wedded the first wife, and He accepted the vow of promise from the man to never leave his wife. And the promise to God was broken and now the prayer of the man is not heard by God. He has turned a deaf ear and ol' boy out there suffering and wondering why God is no longer blessing him.

I'm sure in our modern-day time, if the woman is the one to leave even if the husband is willing to work the marriage out, that the scenario is somewhat the same to a large degree. I'm not male bashing by any means, I am merely going by the biblical text that is directing advice to the men. It goes both ways. Both partners need to be totally committed to the marriage. On the days that the love seems to be dim, the commitment to the marriage will keep you present.

People wonder why their children are going wayward and don't know how to act in public or in the home. But divorce brings turmoil to the lives of the children. They have no godly example to follow because the parents have ended their oneness in divorce. The parents are like human gods to their children. That is who the children should be able to look up to and learn from as they grow in life. A broken home leads to broken children. A broken family with broken people living in separate places. A broken dynamic.

The wife is a gift from God to the husband. Proverbs 19:14 clearly states, "Houses and riches are the inheritance from fathers, but a wise, understanding, and prudent wife is from the Lord." This is God saying to the man that you are not created to do this alone. You need help to further succeed, and I am giving you this wife I designed just for you to help you through your life journey.

"He who finds a wife finds a good thing and obtains favor from the Lord." Proverbs 18:22. Another translation says it like this: "Find a good spouse, you find a good life – and even more: the favor of God! My guess is God takes that favor right back when you decide to divorce, in lieu of showing your spouse understanding, and only giving yourself to your spouse, and to the commitment of your marriage.

It is a miracle and mystery how it happens but somehow God makes the two people become one body. "And the two shall become one flesh; so, they are no longer two, but one flesh." Mark 10:8. This is why divorce must be grieved. It is a true death. Because one person becomes two again; they are split in half. And that hurts. There must be healing, from the trauma and the pain of this type of grieving. And it doesn't matter how many times you divorce; I am a witness that grieving does not get better just because you divorce more than once. In fact, it can be very different circumstances each time and very painful in different ways. But it must be grieved, and any type of grieving of a loss is painful, divorce included.

Understand that God keeps his Word when he makes a covenant with his children. He expects his children to keep their word when they enter a covenant with Him. A covenant is a promise. When you get married you are promising God that you will keep that marriage. It is not a question of should I divorce when hardships arise, it is instead the prayer of asking for wisdom and direction on how to overcome the hardship together and remain in your marriage covenant.

This is how it is supposed to be, however this is not how many of God's children have operated with their marriages. Just like we make the terrible mistake of straying away from our faith, we also may make the terrible mistake of leaving our marriages, and the marriage ends in divorce. I am so glad that God is a forgiving God. I am convinced that the appropriate partner of the ended marriage does reap breaking the covenant between them and God, and if you have a relationship with God you can ask for forgiveness, and God will forgive you. People may not forgive, but God will and does forgive just for asking. Being forgiven is one of the benefits of having a relationship with your Heavenly Father. You can pick up the pieces and try again in this life without condemnation from the Lord.

In the New Testament Jesus teaches about Marriage and Divorce. Mathew 10: 1-10 goes a little something like this:

Modified Bible Story

Jesus was grieving the death of his close cousin John the Baptist. Herod had John the Baptist killed and beheaded and Jesus had to deal with this image in his mind and grieve the loss of his family member who was the one that baptized him!

See what had happened was, Herod did a crazy thing and divorced his wife to marry his half-brother's wife! John the Baptist was preaching in the wilderness to thousands of people and was openly preaching on how wrong Herold was to do what he did. Of course, the new wife didn't like this nor did Herold, so Herod put John the Baptist in prison and later had him beheaded.

Jesus was trying to escape the multitudes of people who were always following him around and trying to get him to heal and teach them. But they wouldn't let up and gave him no peace whatsoever. Jesus was cool so he didn't let the crowd down and would just teach them the righteous way to live their lives and answer their questions.

On this day, the Pharisees, aka the hypocrites, came to Jesus trying to trap him with their question, "should a man be allowed to divorce his wife?"

Jesus in turn asked them a question right back, "What did Moses say about divorce?".

There were multitudes of people standing around waiting for Jesus to answer this question. If Jesus didn't support divorce, then a lot of people in the crowd would dislike him because they were divorced and I'm sure they divorced for the wrong reasons just as Herold had. John the Baptist was dead, and the Pharisees wanted Jesus dead too. Jesus's answer could possibly upset Herold and he would also have Jesus killed, were the hopes of the Pharisees.

The Pharisees answered Jesus saying, Moses permitted divorce, he said a man only has to serve his wife with divorce papers from the court and send her butt away. (Which is totally out of context on how Moses said it).

Jesus said to them, "Moses wrote that in the law only because of their insensitivity to what God has said for them to do. God's plan for marriage was that you never divorce, as it has been seen from the beginning of creation. The man leaves his mother and father and is joined with his wife and the two are permanently united into one. The two become one flesh, they are no longer two, I repeat, one flesh! And the two that are now joined together as one flesh, let no man separate or divide because God has joined them together. But man cannot forgive, and being selfish and self-centered, man wanted a way out of their marriage vows and Moses granted them just that!"

Bam! The Pharisees were left looking stupid again because they didn't trap Jesus at all. Right is right. You can't wrong a right.

When you marry, you need to consider your marriage permanent and govern yourself as such. Don't get married with the thought of getting out if things don't go like you feel they should. Marriage brings oneness to the two. Ephesians 5:32 tell us that how God joins the two as one is a great mystery, but it is much like Christ and the church are one.

Marriage is a vow of forever forgiveness towards your spouse. Patience and long suffering are very necessary in a marriage.

My advice to you is to live by the Biblical guidelines given to you on marriage. Divorce is expensive emotionally, publicly, financially, and even physically. Divorce is a huge loss, and it usually is a result of one or both parties not following the biblical guidelines for the marriage. In other words, not hanging in there for the long haul and working through adversities.

If you have divorced, please take the time to heal and grieve that loss. Whenever you are ready to form a new relationship, I encourage you to do so. And on the contrary, if you meet a potential mate that is healing from divorce, be patient with them and allow them the space and time to heal from the trauma of that division. It's okay to be there for them, and vice versa if you are a divorcee. Everyone is not meant to be alone. Healing does not mean you have to be alone and not have a close friendship as you heal. I am not an advocate for that. I understand that during healing, the enemy can creep in and bring suicidal thoughts, major depression, and illness from the grief.

It is also hard for many people not to continue to contact their ex, and having a close friend can help eliminate that urge. The devil will convince some people to stalk and spy on the ex, even provoke domestic violence and murder. To avoid these detrimental demonic attacks, it may be necessary to allow a close companion to help you through your pain and encourage a more rational thought pattern. It is clear to me that it is not good for some people to be alone and without companionship, especially while experiencing pain from their divorce. However, it is very necessary for the other mate to be understanding, gentle, kind, and very patient through the healing process.

30

CHAPTER 30

MOMMY/DADDY ISSUES

Parenting

I have often heard people say that parenting does not come with a manual. I beg to differ. The Bible is a manual to aid every parent on how to raise their children. There are many scriptures in the Bible that tells us how we should parent. The problem is people don't read manuals.

Society and the environment in which we live may deter us from the advice given in the Bible and that doesn't make it right. Parents have choices, and the choices they make directly affect the children. Some choices affect several descending bloodlines, good and bad choices alike.

The Adult Child

We do not get to choose our parents, or our siblings. God does that for us. The first thing you need to understand is the reason God chose your parents may not ever be revealed to you, however, they were *purposely* chosen by God. You may not like who your Father or Mother is, but you exist because of them, and God *purposely* decided they would be the makeup of your DNA.

The second thing you need to understand is that you are to "Honor (respect, obey, care for) your father and your mother, so that your days may be prolonged in the land the LORD your God gives you." Exodus 20:12 AMP. By honoring your parents as a child and as an adult your days will be prolonged on this Earth as a reward. God is speaking to His children in this verse because He says the "LORD *your* God".

All blessings flow from God above to His children and the last thing you want to do is be disobedient to His instructions on how you should reverence and treat your parents and cut your lifespan short by doing so. At that point what good is your testimony and walking in your Divine Purpose if you don't honor your parents? You diminish the impact your walk with God has on others when you don't honor, and you disrespect your parents. God can't use such an individual that is being blatantly disobedient to His command. When you do not honor and respect your parents you are not living a Kingdom minded lifestyle and you are breaking a commandment given to you by the LORD your God.

Some of the ways you honor your parents is by speaking politely to them and only speaking good of them to others. Always show them respect and be courteous towards them. Why is this important to God that you treat your parents this way? Because HE chose them as your parents with a purpose. It was not their decision. Even when it's difficult for you to honor your parents you are still commanded to do so by God until death. Respect that and live a prolonged life.

Here are some common ways children, including adult children, dishonor their parents.

- Lying to your parents.
- Disobeying your parents.
- Cursing out your parents.
- Speaking evil or harshly of their parents to others.
- Stealing from your parents or taking things without permission.
- Yelling at your parents.
- Walking away from your parents when they are speaking to you.

- Holding a grudge against your parents.
- Cutting off communication or ignoring your parents.
- Blaming your parents for the direction of your own life.
- Talking back and talking rudely to your parents.
- Not taking care of your parents in their time of sickness, old age, or need.
- Making faces, mocking, or rolling your eyes at your parents.
- Complaining about your parents.

Here are some scriptures that will back this up:

Leviticus 20:9: Anyone who curses their father or mother is to be put to death. Because they have cursed their father or mother, their blood will be on their own head.

Mathew 15:4: For God said, 'Honor your father and mother' and anyone who curses their father or mother is to be put to death.'

Proverbs 30:11-13: Some people curse their father and do not thank their mother. They feel pure, but they are filthy and unwashed. They are proud beyond description and disdainful.

Proverbs 30:17: The eye that mocks a father and despises a mother will be plucked out by ravens of the valley and eaten by vultures.

Leviticus 19:32: Show your fear of God by standing up in the presence of elderly people and showing respect for the aged. I am the Lord.

Ephesians 6:2-3: Honor your father and your mother. This is the first commandment with the promise. If you honor your father and mother, things will go well for you, and you will have a long life on earth.

Ephesians 6:1: Children, obey your parents because you belong to the Lord, for this is the right thing to do.

Exodus 21:15: Anyone who strikes their father or mother must be put to death.

Proverbs 15:5: Only a fool despises a parent's discipline; Whoever learns from correction is wise.

Proverbs 23:22: Listen to your father, who gave you life, and don't despise your mother when she is old.

Deuteronomy 21:18-21: Suppose a man has a stubborn and rebellious son who will not obey his father or mother, even though they discipline him. In such a case, the father and mother must take the son to the elders as they hold court at the town gate. The parents must say to the elders, this son of ours is stubborn and rebellious and refuses to obey. He is a glutton and a drunkard. Then all the men of his town must stone him to death. In this way you will purge this evil from among you, and all Israel will hear about it and be afraid.

Colossians 3:20: Children, obey your parents in everything, for this pleases the Lord.

2Timothy 3:2: For people will be lovers of self, lovers of money, proud, arrogant, abusive, disobedient to their parents, ungrateful, unholy,

As you see, it is a large part of wealth building to honor your parents because you are rewarded or blessed by God for doing so. You also get more from your Elders when you show respect towards them, which is also a path towards blessings. The wise Elders will withhold much needed advice from an unruly or rude younger individual because they feel the advice will only fall on deaf ears. Sometimes we need their help or help from their acquaintances, but they will not give the okay to help you because of your disrespectful reputation.

Parenting Your Children

When you become an adult, you should know that your parents did the best they could with what they had within them to parent you. That comes with maturity and age.

Even if they were absent by choice, or by substance, or by illness, which includes mental illness, what they gave as a parent to you was all they could give. What you feel you should have had evidently wasn't what God above felt you should have had as a child. You know this to be true because God will supply all that you need. Not all that you want or think you should have, but all that you need. This includes the type of parent that you were given. You are who you are because of your DNA, your environment, and your upbringing. Including abuse, God knew what type of parent you would have, and He used them to shape and mold you into who you are today whether they were present or not, loving, or abusive, you were assigned those parents for a reason that you cannot change.

A lot of times people say that they will parent differently than how their parents parented them and it's nothing wrong with that. Life is a learning journey. Just know most children will find something wrong with the way they were raised and that will include yours!

Nevertheless, you do the best you can to raise your children according to the Biblical guidelines set before you. If you have a child or children that grow up feeling as though you were not a good parent and you know you did the best you could, leave it in God's hands. The enemy will use your children to deter you from walking in your purpose. All you can do is pray for them, not become consumed with sorrow, and keep walking towards your destiny. The past cannot be changed and grown children holding on to the past without working that out within themselves or with a professional are showing signs of immaturity. As mature adults we should have a mature level of love, understanding, forgiveness, compassion, and acceptance, especially for our parents.

I love my parents. My childhood story is not a pleasant story, however, as an adult it is very important to me to maintain a loving and present relationship with my parents. It is important to me to love, honor, and respect my parents. For myself, I forgave them for whatever I felt they did or did not do correctly in my life. I exist because of them and for that I am grateful.

Scriptures On Parenting

Again, the scriptures are a tool and guideline to living a successful life. It also says to obey the laws of the land. There is a difference between discipline and abuse. The Bible is not saying to abuse your children when it speaks of "sparing the rod". It is simply saying that children need consequences for wrongful behaviors to learn what is right and what is wrong.

There are plenty of ways to discipline a child without abusing them. Proverbs 23:13-14 says, "Don't fail to correct your children. They won't die if you spank them. Physical discipline may well save them from death."

Parents fear disciplining their children in these times and that's unfortunate because discipline keeps the children from ending up in situations that may lead them to incarceration or possibly death. Parenting is not being a friend to your child. Friends don't discipline because they have no authority over the other person. Parents represent an authoritative figure in the life of their children. When the parent is not seen as an authoritative role model, there is a problem within the dynamic of the parent/child relationship.

Proverbs 22:6 says, "Teach your children to choose the right path, and when they are older, they will remain upon it."

The Bible also tells us, "Foolishness is bound up in the heart of a child, but the rod of correction will drive it far from him." This will tell you why we have so many foolish adults walking the Earth. More than likely, there was a breakdown in their parent/child dynamic growing up.

The goal of a parent should be to raise law abiding, mature, dependable, responsible adults who live their lives according to the Word of God. The Word of God is not for us to be wrapped up in tradition or religious rituals, but a true map of how to navigate through life while sustaining a relationship with the Creator.

Correcting our children is loving our children just as much as reading to them, singing to them, and playing with them is loving them. Proverbs 13:24 says, "He who spares his rod of discipline hates his children, but he who loves them disciplines diligently and punishes them early."

There is a reason why the Bible speaks to the parent in so many scriptures to discipline the children. Check out these scriptures:

Don't trust anyone—not your best friend or even your wife! For the son despises his father. The daughter defies her mother. The daughter-in-law defies her mother-in-law. Your enemies will be right in your own household. Micah 7:5-6.

The father shall be divided against the son, and the son against the father; the mother against the daughter, and the daughter against the mother; the mother-in-law against her daughter-in-law and the daughter-in-law against her mother-in-law. Luke 12:53.

Brother will deliver brother over to death, and the father his child, and the children will rise against parents and have them put to death, Mathew 10:21

There will be division and strife within the immediate family. There's no need to be shocked that sons are against their fathers and do not like, love, or care for their fathers. There's no need to be shocked that daughters are against their mothers and do not like, do not love, do not care for their mother. It is in the Bible that this will be so. So many people talk about the mother daughter relationship and the lack of a father and son relationship, but if you pay attention to what it says in the Word of God it tells you this is how it will be. And it says it over and over!

The biggest and greatest way to try to prevent this from happening is by staying with the family dynamic according to the Word of God. And even then, there will be strife between the parent and the child. Absent parents affect children negatively. Children witnessing their parents divorcing at any age is traumatic for them. Children with absent parents grow up not knowing how to be a parent themselves or how to be a husband or wife to their spouse because that example was not present in their own life. Even when they are parents, they over parent and use less or incorrect discipline trying hard not to be like the parents they had.

There are very few children growing up with their biological mother and father, until they bury their parents who died still married and together. Few people are blessed with that example and if you are one of those people, please thank your parents for hanging in there and overcoming obstacles together and honoring their vows of marriage. The world has made divorce so easy. Staying married for a lifetime is very hard to do and very rare. This is so unfortunate.

All you can do as a parent is your very best. A grand outcome is not guaranteed. The Bible tells us that for sure. Situations are different and all marriages can't be saved, all parents can't be present. We just aren't perfect people. We make mistakes as people and that includes raising our children. We can hope that our children grow up and understand that we did our best within our ability to do, and hope that they love us anyway.

I'm pretty sure this is why the Bible advises us not to commit adultery, not to fornicate, and why God hates divorce. The outcome will more than likely end up in a jacked-up family dynamic that damages the people involved. I am even a part of a family where the father has several baby mamas. Some of my siblings have little to no relationship with my father or one another.

No matter how hard my dad tried to be a father to all his children, the fact that they had different mothers, and different households played a factor in diminishing his efforts to be a father. The children will most likely suffer in some way in such situations, and so will the parent/child relationship, it's no way around it.

The hardships experienced in so many mother/daughter relationships are not a generational curse. The strained father/son relationship is not a generational curse. Generational curses can be broken but unfortunately the Bible tells us that this family breakdown in relationships between children and their parents will happen. Many mothers are going to have a hard time with their daughters. Many fathers are going to have a hard time with their sons. I searched for an answer to this problem and what I came up with was "love, forgiveness, and time".

Not honoring your parents is a sin, regardless of what you feel they did or did not do. The Bible tells us that love covers a multitude of sins. Not just regular love, but that 1Corinthians chapter 13 type love. A Godly love. It is going to take forgiveness for the mistakes made by both the children and parents alike. It is going to take patience and time to develop the spiritual growth that is necessary to apply towards healing, and finding the type of love that forgives takes time and maturity. Not everybody makes it to this point. But now that **you** know better, **you** are required to do better as you head towards your journey of success because it will hinder you in some way if you don't. (Even if they are deceased, you must make peace, forgive, and honor them in your heart, with your actions and with your words).

My relationship with my mom as a young child was strained until I was well into my adult years, and I learned this concept that I have shared with you, and I forgave her. I love her, and it is very important to me to maintain a respectful relationship with her. It is in my heart to have this with her. I have one mother that gave birth to me. I had to do the same with my father. I don't know or have a relationship with all my siblings, but I love my father and maintaining a respectful heartfelt relationship with him is very important to me. I forgive him for the things I felt he did wrong by me, and I understand it may not have been wrong to him at all. He is the parent, and I respect that.

God chose my parents to create **me**. I also humbly respect that.

Learn how to love correctly, with a Godly 1Corithians chapter 13, filled with the fruits of the Spirit. Love and teach your children how to love the same way, always leading by example.

31

CHAPTER 31

THE POWER COUPLE

If your desire is to be a power couple with your mate, then finding the right mate for you may be more taxing and exhausting than you thought it would be if you are currently single. If you are already married, there must be a certain mindset of your mate for your union to become a power couple.

In the power couple dynamic, it must be two confident and secure individuals with clear and precise visions for themselves. The visions align because the two respect and understand the visions of the other and allow the spouse the opportunity and space to achieve their goals and assist when necessary. Some share the same vision and can work together on that particular vision. No one negates their vision to allow the other to achieve theirs. Both simultaneously work on achieving their goals and visions. This requires unselfishness from both parties.

The power couple is made up of two chosen people walking in their divine purpose. They already know what their gifts, dreams, and aspirations are, coupled with their faith and determination individually. When the two join as one and remain as focused and driven as they were individually, if not even more so, this creates the power couple.

If a Chosen vessel marries unequally yoked, you cannot and will not become a power couple because only one is Chosen. There will be too many missing spiritual components in the union. The Bible warns against being unequally yoked because God wants His Chosen children to fulfill their purpose for their creation. Marrying unequally yoked will prove to be a hinderance in accomplishing that.

Individually, chosen people suffer demonic attacks just because they are chosen by and on a mission for God. Imagine the impact of demonic attacks against a power couple! Two C hosen people that became one in matrimony bring a tremendous force naturally and spiritually. This is why the power couple is a rarity. The demonic attacks are so fierce, clever, and forceful, it takes a special bonding to withstand them and remain as one.

If you are single and desire to be a power couple, you need to start now with preparing your mind, body, and spirit for that. Chosen people should not be fornicators. When you fornicate, you are creating soul ties and taking on the demonic characteristics or infestations of the individual that you are having sex with. And if they are having sex with other people, you are also being infested with the demonic characteristics of the people your sex partner is sleeping with. These demonic infestations will show up when you are married because it is the purpose of the devil to end your marriage. These demonic spirits will lay dormant until you are married and then manifest themselves to wreak havoc on your marriage until it has ended in separation or divorce. And that is the end of the power couple.

The devil does not want you to be a power couple with your spouse. So before getting married I suggest you cleanse yourself of all soul ties and fill that void with the Holy Spirit so that it is not left empty. If it is left empty, then Satan is coming right back in somehow. Cleansing is done through prayer by asking God to cast out all unclean and demonic infestations that you received from fornication, with whatever else you choose to incorporate. Such as throwing out all gifts or things that were given to you, destroying, or deleting any photos, etc. If you are currently married and have not done this, please do so immediately and watch how behaviors and characteristics improve.

The 90/10 Rule

The Bible is written for Believers. It is only on rare occasions that non-believers will read the Bible. Many people are believers but don't study the Word of God. There are many believers who are walking in their Divine purpose, and still don't study the Word of God.

Then we have those people who are descendants of a favored and blessed ancestry that reap the blessings of those in their bloodline, and they appear to be Chosen, but are just descendants of a blessed linage. Because of the prayers and obedience of the linage before them, God keeps His promise to their forefathers and/or mothers and continues to bless their forthcoming generations. This is not just with material gain, but also with knowledge and a degree of worldly wisdom. Godly wisdom, the Spirit of Wisdom, only comes from the studying and the reading of the Word.

You, the Chosen Vessel, need to be able to discern different types of believers and where they are spiritually. This will not only help you in seeking Godly counsel and advice, but in selecting a mate. It is ideal for a Chosen vessel to be married to another Chosen vessel and become a Power Couple. It is ideal, but not mandatory or necessary. Some believers may have been created just to be the support and back bone to their Chosen spouse.

Nevertheless, you need to be able to know and discern where other believers are in their walk with Christ and what kind of mate is best for you.

In many cases, the single Chosen few have a horrible time when it comes to dating and finding a suitable mate. When you have goals and aspirations you are pushing towards, not only is your way of doing things and how you move different from the norm, but your time is different. The entire way you view time is different. You have no time for dating just to hang out because you have too many purposes that need your attention. The biggest problem with that is the average believer will not understand that concept. Their mind can't grasp this concept because they are not operating on the same dimension. They just feel you don't have the time allotted to give to them or you are all about yourself.

The beauty of a Chosen vessel dating and marrying another Chosen vessel Is the understanding of the grind, the thought process, and the time management. This should cut down on the whining, the nagging, and the accusing. It should bring forth a broader spectrum which includes praying for one another in your absence and understanding the quality of the time spent rather than the quantity.

The Chosen are the few...so one Chosen finding another Chosen as a mate is not all that easy. But in trusting God, you know it will happen. It Just won't happen overnight.

One day I was praying about this and asking God about my mate, and He told me He is a God of one tenth. Then He proceeded to show me what He meant in regard to a mate.

Only 10% of believers are Chosen. Only 10% of believers walk in their Divine purpose. That leaves 90%. Which brings me to the 90/10 Rule.

God told me my mate is not in the 90%, my mate is in the 10%. I have been looking for a mate in the 90% and this has caused me a lot of heartache and divorce. Just because the person has a good profession and nice income does not make them a part of the 10%, it does not mean they are a part of the Chosen few. Being Chosen is a heart and spiritual matter. You will know them by the fruits that they bear. Mathew 7:16.

It's so easy to go to the 90% because that's where the abundance of eligible people are found. But a Chosen looking for another Chosen is like looking for the needle in the haystack. It's doable, but harder and takes a lot more time.

A common mistake that is made with a single Chosen vessel is the decision to remain single as they walk in their purpose. The two are always better than the one. It is not good that man be alone. You can accomplish so much more with the right individual by your side. Being single and Chosen opens the doorway to sin and distractions.

However, the experience of the trauma from having a relationship with someone in the 90% brings discouragement in finding the proper mate and a person may decide being single is the best option. If this is your mindset, I encourage you to explore the option of finding a mate within the 10%, and once that person is in your life so many more doors will open for you. That is the promise to the man that finds a good wife, God will bless him with favor. **You can't get that favor being single**. Part of creating wealth is using your intelligence and maximizing **all** the avenues God has laid before you. If a man chooses not to marry, he will not receive all the favor and blessings God has in store for him. This, my friend, is a key to greater success. Proverbs 18:22.

Look for the Chosen believer whose mindset aligns with what you need in your life. These people understand how to love with 1Corithians chapter 13 type love. These people are walking in their purpose and are goal oriented. These people are praising God in the sanctuary. These people are Kingdom minded. These people will outwardly pray for and with you! These people are different from the norm.

Some Chosen knew they were Chosen from childhood. And others came to Christ and the Royal Priesthood as an adult, and then they started operating in their Divine purpose. Both instances make up the 10%, be mindful of a Chosen vessel new to the 10% and allow them the time needed to develop and grow.

32

CHAPTER 32

ADVICE TO KEEP THE ENEMY AT BAY

Ignoring the Love Language

If you are not fulfilling the love language of your spouse, it is likely they will find what they are needing from you in someone else. I am not saying this behavior is right, I'm just saying it is how affairs can get started. It's imperative that you keep your spouse full of what they need from you to feed their love language. Looking for attention, touch, quality time, etc. outside of your spouse is a hinderance to becoming a power couple or maintaining power couple status.

You can't achieve mutual goals with outside distractions lingering around. It's a trick from the enemy to keep couples from succeeding in God's plan for their bonded lives. Conquer and divide. Most times when the spouse has gone outside of the union, separation, and divorce creeps in, and Satan has one up.

The intelligent way to keep this from happening is by learning what your spouse's love language is and keeping their tank full of what they need. Compliment your mate often and do nice little surprises for them. If your mate is asking for more intimacy or alone time, it is necessary to find ways to make that happen. For example, if quality time is their love language and you are consumed with work, or raising the children, someone else will eventually get their attention and provide them with the time and attention you are not providing. Then they are labeled the cheater and scum of the earth, but what were the circumstances that opened the door for someone else to walk in? Were you, the spouse, giving them the time and attention they needed? Therefore, it is also you who is at fault. Their actions may have been the consequences of your not providing or giving what your spouse needed from you. I'm just saying.

Some cliches have a lot of truth to them, and in this case, here are two that seem relevant: "what one won't do, the other one will" and "it takes two to tangle".

Cheating

Cheating is not just sexual intercourse. Cheating is inappropriate conversations, and attachments outside of your spouse.

Cheating is not paying household bills when expected to do so by your spouse and carelessly spending the money elsewhere.

Cheating is giving sums of money to another adult outside of the household without your spouse's consent.

Cheating is leaving without your spouse knowing your whereabouts and ignoring your spouse's calls and attempts to contact you.

Cheating is not being open and engaging in honest communication with your spouse in attempts to repair or improve the broken components of your marriage.

The distraction Satan throws into your marriage is not always in the form of another individual. However, it is all equally wrong and damaging. Prayers are hindered at this point because the prayers are now different. They are prayers of reconciliation instead of two bonded as one praying for continued success and prosperity within the marriage. Which is the prayer of the power couple. The team is divided, bitterness and hurt has set in, now the goals as a power couple must come to a halt until reconciliation can take place. Or worse, the goals are never accomplished because division and divorce take their wrongful place in the lives of the once bonded pair.

Not Doing the Work

Nothing good comes easily. Another truth. Marriage within itself is hard work. It is harder than a nine to five job that pays you a paycheck. Marriage requires individual change and individual self-work. You cannot change the other person, only yourself, and you must change throughout the course of your marriage with each new step or new level, individually.

If the two are not willing to change, it will make for a rocky marriage. One person working on their own self is not enough. One is not married to oneself. It takes the two to put in the hard work to make a successful marriage.

The difference between a power couple and a marriage that has stood the test of time is the work put into the marriage and the willingness to change. A marriage can last with no one changing or putting in the work. It just means that they stay together and just endure what is being dished out by the other partner. It looks like to the outsiders that the marriage is successful. But in fact, at least one of the two has a broken heart that eventually hardens. They then just become numb to the injustice in the marriage and remain legally committed.

But a power couple operates so differently, which makes them so few and so rare in this day and age. The power couple has goals to achieve as a couple. By viewing the marriage somewhat similar to that of a business or corporation, they understand change and compromise individually is a necessary ingredient for success in achieving their financial and personal goals. Constant communication, meetings, embedded with pure honesty, truth, loyalty, dedication, transparency, and determination to succeed is what each member must bring to the meetings of this power merger.

Ignoring the Corporation Idealization

The president is the husband, and the vice president is the wife. Nothing is ever done by either without the others' consent or knowledge or approval. Something very small is enough to create a problem within the progress of the company. The time it will take to correct the problem is time that could have been used to propel the couple forward towards their mutual goals. There is not even room for outsiders to have an opinion on how the two run this corporate union. That can also cause discourse in marriage.

Advice and counsel can be given, and should be welcomed when mutually agreed upon, but only from reputable resources. All advice and counsel that includes changes in activities should be to benefit the two as one and both should work towards improving their merger and lifestyle as one. No time for slacking or being halfway invested or not invested at all. It is goals to achieve and prosperity to obtain as a couple.

The power couple is committed to the long haul of the success of the marriage. Both are willing to be forgiving, and understanding, and patient, as understanding entrepreneurs of their union. Both are willing to always give 100% to matrimony which includes working on positive self-improvements and changes to empower the success of the marriage.

What the other spouse needs to feel loved, wanted and mutually goal oriented, each spouse provides for the other. It sounds easy, but it's hard work.

Hard work and perseverance always pay positive dividends. So please do the work!

Not Making Your Spouse Your Priority

Your spouse must be your priority. Let nothing and no one come in between you and your spouse. Only God is greater. Not your job, not your kids, not your parents, not your siblings, not your pastor, nothing and no one on earth is before your spouse.

It is no one's business what takes place in your household. Do not air out your dirty laundry. Work those things out privately with your spouse. Do not speak negatively to others of your spouse and do not tell lies to others concerning your spouse, and do not lie to your spouse. Lying is an ugly sin and opens the door for Satan to walk right into your marriage and destroy it.

Write your business plans together. Write your mutual goals together, and together chart your successes towards your goals. Celebrate as often as you can together. Celebrate small things and small achievements together, celebrate important dates and holidays together. Vow to never be apart on those important days. This is encouraging, keeps you happy, and strengthens the marriage.

Try to have weekly discussions, call them board meetings, and discuss all aspects of your union and lives together with honesty. Share likes and dislikes because we change over time. Our needs and wants can change as well. Share everything with one another. As best friends in matrimony should.

No one is perfect, we must allow our spouse room for mistakes. Both should learn from their mistakes and have no intention of repeating them. Avoid saying sorry and there is no change in actions or attitude.

Consider a power couple contract. I call it a power couple contract because it takes an elevated mentality to understand the purpose of such a contract within a union.

Not Enduring Until the End

This race is not given to the swift nor the strong, but to the one who endures to the end. This is not a Bible verse, yet so relevant and true. I haven't made it into ripe old age with the same spouse just yet, but I can only imagine the type of bond, love, connection, and joy this couple must have with one another after enduring and staying together through the test of time.

To remain a power couple, you must endure the trials and tribulations within the marriage, with your spouse. Win the race together. It will draw you closer and strengthen your bond. This may not be your first marriage, but this can be the marriage that lasts and makes you a part of the winners' matrimony circle. The power couple that succeeded and achieved lifetime prosperity together. Best friends for life! Until death does you two apart.

Don't just be a married couple, be a power couple and merge your goals, creativity, and ideas for your Divine Destinations. Together you should work hard for your combined success.

Commit and vow to the union, as well as to God, to never leave the other spouse. Do not tolerate mistreatment or abuse of any kind. Get help and support for those behaviors and allow room for change if it is possible. Forgive mistakes, that's different from continued abuse or mistreatment.

Welcome the changes and efforts to change by your spouse. Allow room and patience for that, change is not overnight. But effort is continual and should be rewarded with praise, patience, and understanding.

Do not speak of divorce or separation, because what you say may materialize. Then you will have regrets and pain. This is a pain you don't know until you have experienced it. You do not want to experience this pain.

33

CHAPTER 33

THE POWER COUPLE CONTRACT

God has clearly told us that fornication is a part of sexual immorality and a sin. A Relationship Contract is normally a contract between two people who are not married but in a committed relationship that includes sexual activities. I cannot advocate for a Relationship Contract for this reason.

However, I do advocate for a Matrimony Contract and in this case, I came up with a Power Couple Contract. (I came up with Matrimony Contract as well, because even if only one spouse is operating in their Divine purpose they are still set apart from worldly practices.) I see the Power Couple Contract being different from a Matrimony Contract because of the higher dimensional level of **two** Chosen individuals in a marriage together.

Chosen people are not the average, normal type individuals. Chosen people are different, understand differently, and move differently from the average individual. 1 Peter 2:9 puts it like this: "But you are a CHOSEN RACE, A royal PRIESTHOOD, A HOLY NATION, A PEOPLE FOR God's OWN POSESSION, so that you may proclaim the excellencies of Him who has called you out of darkness into His marvelous light;" There is absolutely nothing normal about this type of a Holy Nation. Therefore, a contract between the couple is not the normal contract for a regular marriage. There is no way this marriage union can be "regular". It is rare, unique, and different from the norm.

To have a Power Couple Contract that fits your marriage, it must be tailored towards your goals, needs, and wants as a Chosen couple. There are some components that will look similar on every contract and some that will not.

It is wise to be able to express to your spouse your specific needs and desires and comforting to know that security will be provided for you. Doing this in written form will help eliminate arguments, disagreements, misunderstandings, miscommunication, and resentful feelings that will hinder the progress of your mutual wealth building process. By creating this power couple contract together, you will get a clear indication of what your spouses' needs and wants are. You won't have to guess or worry about not giving what they need or what is expected of you.

The Power Couple Contract opens the window for transparency and communication and sets the tone for those key components to continue throughout the union. It will also provide a guideline and timeline for mutual goals set by the two of you. The Power Couple Contract is the vision for the marriage. Your vision is the key towards creating and maintaining Power Couple status. "Write the vision; make it plain...it hastens toward the goal, and it will not fail..." Habakkuk 2:2-3.

If followed by each spouse effectually, The Power Couple contract will prove to be one of the greatest assets towards a very successful couple.

It doesn't matter if you have already been married or just getting married, once you come upon this revelation of the importance of The Power Couple Contract or even the Matrimony Contract, sit down with your spouse and give each other a time frame to think about what should be on the contract to fit the needs of the individual as well as the couple, and then in a calm, romantic setting, write it out. If you need help forming this contract, contact my team and someone will help you through it and even draw it up for you.

The contract is an agreement and promise between the two of you and not binding by law. It is merely an intentional tool for the success of the marriage, as the marriage matures and changes. As the goals are being met, priorities and needs change. New goals and new needs arise. Therefore, the contract needs to be reviewed and revised periodically. I suggest the first contract be reviewed after the first 90 days. Then decide together if you should review it every 90 days, 6 months, or a year moving forward. Allow the time set aside to review and make changes to the contract to be separate from date nights, vacations, and personal intimate times. View the timing as a business meeting with your business partner and have it in a calming and serene atmosphere.

There will be those that will oppose doing such a contract. It is my opinion that these type people are non-committal and non-transparent. You cannot be a power couple without total commitment and full transparency.

CHAPTER 34

CONTRACT CONTENT

1. Each individual needs to write out how they are taking responsibility for their own health, mental growth, physical growth, personal growth, emotional growth, gifts, and talents. It is expected this part of the contract will often change during the contract review periods.
2. Being that it is not anyone else's responsibility to make you happy, each individual needs to be responsible for their own happiness. Write out what this will look like for both parties separately on the contract.
3. Agree on how much time can be spent with friends, personal independent time, and hobbies without the other spouse. Also, include the frequency of vacation trips with friends that exclude the spouse, if any.
4. Independent chores and household responsibilities need to be defined. Include alternating chores and chores done together as a team.
5. How you treat and address each other respectfully, especially during times of conflict, needs to be defined as well as the tone and language used when addressing one another.
6. How you will spend holidays, special dates, special occasions, and celebrations of accomplishments needs to be listed. It is my opinion to

try to spend all of the holidays, birthdays, and anniversaries together to keep resentment from arising, and vacation together at least once a year, and with kids at least once a year if you have children. Two vacations a year if you have children and the family vacation needs to be the shorter vacation between the two separate vacations. At least one vacation a year if you don't have children.

7. Agree to never keep secrets from one another and never lie to each other.

8. Set days and length of time for dates between the two of you, and time allotted for business talks of the goals and aspirations each one is working towards. I suggest weekly dates and weekly business talks outside of date night.

9. Agree and write out what is expected with sexual intimacy and how often.

10. Write out boundaries and what is acceptable when it comes to other people, as far as touching, hugging, conversations, alone time, etc.

11. Agree on how to settle disagreements and not to go to bed angry. Call time outs with an I love you and embrace.

12. Write out what each partner needs emotionally and physically from the other partner, within reason, and come to mutual terms of agreement as to how often.

13. Also write out what is needed from the other partner to help with the others' goals, ministry, and business adventures.

14. Agree on getting consent from the other partner before giving money to others over a certain dollar amount. You can also set a limit on how much to spend on gifts for each other and others outside of the marriage.

15. Agree to not divorce or separate or threaten this action at any time.

16. If you plan to have children, agree on when within the contract and agree on pregnancy prevention.

17. Agree on the time frame of the notice given to the other spouse on business trips and business ventures.

18. Write out how the bills will be paid, who will handle each financial responsibility, and how the bank accounts will be set up. Agree on a dollar amount that can be spent without the knowledge or mutual consent of the other spouse. Anything over that dollar amount requires

the agreement of both spouses.

19. Each spouse needs to write out the individual goals and achievements they are working towards and give a time frame for completion or specific achievements. Then write out the aspirations for achievement as a couple, the input role of each partner in achieving that aspiration and a milestone within the journey of achievement and how the two will celebrate that milestone together.

20. Both parties sign The Power Couple Contract and date it.

Since there should not be a separation or divorce, I suggest not adding the terms or penalties for that to this type of contract. Instead draw up a prenup, and if you are already married, then you can sign a postnuptial agreement. Prenups and Postnuptial contracts are lawfully binding and need to be notarized.

After reading things that should be included in The Power Couple Contract, you can now see how it really does eliminate a lot of extra heartache, especially insecurities that can arise. Most Chosen people have professions that have them around a lot of influential people and it's easy for the spouse to become jealous or insecure within the married relationship. But knowing and trusting your spouse adheres to the terms of the agreement written out between the two of you helps keep all that extra strife at bay. It gives the enemy less room to play with the battlefield of the mind.

A major key is that neither spouse purposely does anything that will invite more adversity into the marriage than the couple is already going to face. The main key is staying together through all adversity and keeping a loving relationship.

CHAPTER 35

PROVERBS 31

Proverbs 31 is said to be about the Virtuous Woman. I feel Proverbs 31 is about a woman who is a part of a Power Couple. The passage clearly says her husband is famous and she is a working entrepreneur herself walking in her Divine Destiny with her husband's approval and praises. That's a Power Couple.

King Soloman wrote the book of Proverbs in fact he wrote about 3000 proverbs, 1000 songs, and several books of the Bible. I do believe King Lemuel is the name King Solomon's mom referred to him by because Proverbs 31 is the advice from the King's mother on what kind of woman he should have. Many believe this is the advice Bathsheba gave to Soloman who had woman troubles. He had 700 wives and 300 concubines. His mother saw that his downfall was his love for multiple women and drinking. If he had the "right *one* woman" then he wouldn't need all those wrong women that obviously didn't satisfy his appetite. So often, even though we are chosen and have an awesome relationship with our God, we chose the wrong mate and end up in bad relationships.

Solomon married women that God specifically told the Israelites not to marry because these women served other gods and would have the men of God serving other gods as well. Solomon, the wisest man of his time, did not take heed to God's instructions when it came to females. As a result, Solomons wives did to him exactly what God said they would do, and Solomon brought the country to a lot of strife, and he eventually grew cold towards God. You can't be fully devoted to the God of Heaven and His purpose for your life and marry someone that serves false gods, and they aren't living a righteous lifestyle.

The woman that gave the advice in Proverbs 31 was the mother of a King. She understood, through experience and wisdom, how a woman chosen by God and walking in her Divine purpose, would be the perfect match for a Chosen man of God who is also walking in his divine purpose. Which would give us what we call today, the "Power Couple".

This was her advice to her son, the King. It was an example; it was not a real woman. However, it lets us know that the mother giving the advice to the son must be this type of woman to know what advice to give her son. Trials, mistakes, and life's experiences had to give her this wisdom to grow into such a woman herself, for the mother of a King had to once be married to a King and be Queen herself!

Bathsheba is Solomon's mother. Before Bathsheba became King David's wife, she was the wife of Uriah who was the general of David's army. Before Bathsheba was the influential queen to David, she was the understanding, strong wife of a general. Not just any woman can fill either one of those roles. David had a harem of women, and none of them could measure up to his captivation with Bathsheba.

Bathsheba slept with David and committed adultery while married to Uriah and got pregnant by David. This was during a time that women, not men, women were stoned for committing adultery, yet Bathsheba was never considered for such fate. That's God's favor.

But she had to mourn the death of her husband, who was killed by the Kings orders. David tried to get Uriah to go home and sleep with Bathsheba so he would think it was his baby she was carrying. Uriah was loyal to the servants of David and wouldn't sleep in his bed with Bathsheba while the servants had to sleep in tents, instead he slept in the tents with the servants. David gave the order to kill Uriah by putting him on the front line of the enemy's fire on the battlefield.

Because of King Davids lust for Bathsheba, she lost her husband to an early death, and it hurt. The Bible said she mourned for her husband, Uriah. David waited until her time of mourning was over and he sent for her, and she then became David's wife. Imagine the shame attached to her mourning, and on top of that, her baby died. God told David that what he had done was evil and the baby would not live. The baby lived 7 days and died. I wrote a song about how Bathsheba must have felt when this happened to her. My lyrics are sung by Dr. Juanita Fletcher. Listen to it when you have a chance.

King David and Bathsheba had a special bond, she was different from the harem of women King David had. Not one of those women could measure up to be a Queen to the King. She was set apart from the harem and was loved by King David who made Bathsheba his Queen, and they had another baby together, the wisest King to ever walk the Earth, King Solomon.

The fact that Bathsheba could tell her son how the woman in Proverbs 31 operated her business, her marriage, her children, and her home, let's me know that Bathsheba herself was this kind of woman. She was a power couple when she was married to Uriah. Uriah was a general in David's army, he was not a poor man. Uriah and Bathsheba lived in a mansion with a rooftop hot tub and that's where David saw her bathing. When David married her, she was still a part of a power couple dynamic when she became Queen to King David. Bathsheba did not go from rags to riches, she went from rich to richer. And her own skills and talents keep her busy while each husband attended to their purpose and calling. With all this going on I'm more than positive the women of the town had a lot of names and gossip going on concerning Bathsheba.

King David found Bathsheba beautiful. Take note that King David had a harem of beautiful women. Something else made King David want Bathsheba in his bed so much that he couldn't keep his eyes off of her. It was not the outward beauty that captivated him to summon for, and sleep with, his loyal general's wife. It was her character as a woman, it was the ultimate wife she was to her husband, it was her creativity and drive to work towards her passions, it was her obedience to walk in her purpose, it was her position with God, it was the favor of God on this woman's life. Outward appearance cannot touch such characteristics because it is rare to find this type of woman. David was told exactly whose wife Bathsheba was. He knew of what type of wife Uriah had, he must have heard the praises Uriah would brag of his adorable wife, and that's why David sent for her.

King Solomon was like most men today, that consistently entertain the women that God says for them not to be involved with, and instead they overlook, and dismiss the "virtuous woman" God is gifting them with. Even though King Solomon's mom gave him the advice on what type of woman to find, he still did not listen. Some people just will not listen to Wisdom when she speaks. You can lead a horse to the water, but you cannot make him drink.

The woman described in Proverbs 31 was very talented, skillful, wise, and an incredible businesswoman, mother, and wife. I believe Bathsheba could mention all those things the virtuous woman did, because she herself did them all. This woman Bethsheba describes was compassionate, and her husband had nothing but good things to say about her and **he trusted her**. Trust is so important in a Power Couple dynamic.

It is clear to me that Bathsheba supported and was a backbone or rib to both of her husbands. This woman gave her son this advice on the type of woman he needed to marry because she had the same characteristics, and she knew from experience. It had to bring a woman of her knowledge, her wisdom, and her statue in God, great pain to watch her son go from female to female to female and have an alcohol problem. He could have had so much more if he had chosen just the right "one" and gave his all to that one wife.

This is my version of what Proverbs 31 is saying:

1. This is the story that King Solomon, aka Lemuel, told of how his mom tried to tell him to leave the hundreds of females and the alcohol alone. But he didn't listen and now years later, he wishes he had. It would have saved him a lot of trouble.

2. Listen to me, son. Do not continue to ignore me, I carried you inside me for almost 10 months, and I got pregnant with you while I was married to your father, you are not a bastard child. You are the product of a marriage, and your mother and father raised you, yet you are out here acting like you had no home training.

3. You need to leave those no-good females alone. They can only bring harm to your judgment and your reputation. You are a King for Pete's sake!

4. And Lemuel, you need to stop all that drinking and getting drunk you are doing! Kings are men of high regard, and they have no business dealing with an alcohol addiction and parading around drinking beer in public.

5. Kings can't make good judgment calls for the kingdom if they are tipsy or drunk. Then the people of the kingdom will suffer because of bad decisions their King made while he was intoxicated.

6. Let people who have nothing to live for drink beer and strong alcohol and let people who have heavy hearts with grief try to numb their pain with wine,

7. Let the homeless and the poor and those who have no aspirations or high positions in life drink away their sorrows.

8. You are charged with making major decisions for the people of our kingdom and representing the people who can't stand up for themselves.

9. You need to be sober minded to make these types of decisions, and to be able to make fair judgement calls. You cannot be intoxicated when you defend the rights of those who need you.

10. Son, why haven't you found a good wife? That's what you need, having a good wife is more valuable than any amount of money you could make.

11. A good wife has the trust of her husband. He knows she won't be out in other men's faces or in other men's bed, and she will make sure her husband has everything he needs.

12. Her mission will be to comfort, encourage, support, and never mistreat her husband until death due them apart.

13. A good wife doesn't mind working and running businesses to help build the storehouse with her husband. She's not a gold digger, son.

14. She is an international entrepreneur and understands her business is not limited to just her city or country.

15. She's up in the wee hours of the morning running her business and making money for her household and doing payroll to pay the employees of the companies. And she still makes time to cook breakfast for her children and her husband to get their day started after doing all of that.

16. To prevent her husband from being disturbed while working, she will take the tedious steps to go house hunting and find the perfect land and home for the family. Then she will make sure the gardening and the upkeep of the property is well maintained so her husband can be free to work on his endeavors.

17. She exercises and works out to keep her body in shape, her health intact, and her muscles toned.

18. Even at night she makes sure the businesses are running proficiently, and she will get up and handle any issue that needs attention without hesitation.

19. She can make and design clothes if she needs to. She can take a plain T-Shirt and make it look like an expensive top.

20. She is kind and generous, does charity events, and helps the less fortunate.

21. A little chill outside doesn't bother her or keep her from going out and handling business because she has plenty of coats and clothes to keep her and her family warm.

22. Not cheap clothing either, she wears quality clothing and always looks nice when she steps outside of the house.

23. This is the wife of a well-known, respectable, wealthy, businessman, who has wise friends in high places.

24. She has a boutique in malls and/or online where she sells nice clothes and accessories.

25. She is an honorable woman that is held in high regards. She doesn't worry about the days ahead because she knows through faith and hard work, she and her family will have a promising future.

26. Her way of speaking is gentle yet full of wisdom and knowledge.

27. She does not entertain gossiping, low self-esteem, self-pity, or being lazy. She is always busy doing something productive in a cheerful manner.

28. Her children think the world of her and know they have the best mom and example God could provide them. Her husband adores her and knows no woman out there can bring him the joy that she does.

29. Her husband tells her, there are many female businesswomen out there, but none can hold a candle to you in my eyesight!

30. Many women charm men into marrying them to take care of them and they do not have their husbands' best interests in their hearts. And these men fall for such women because they feel the women are beautiful and will look good on their arms. You need a woman of God that is delighting herself in the Lord always because she will be good to you and be the mate that God wants you to have. This is a true praiseworthy woman.

31. This is the type of woman that deserves a good man. This woman is who she is because she earned her position, and all that she possesses, with hard work, faith in God, and perseverance.

Bathsheba used her influence as King David's favorite and closest wife to get Solomon the position as King. Solomon was not next in line for that position. But Solomon had the heart of his father, King David. He watched how his father loved the Lord and prayed to God for direction. Solomon followed his father's example and developed a strong relationship with the Lord.

God asked Solomon what gift he wanted, and Solomon asked for wisdom to rule wisely in his position as King. This reveals where Solomon's heart was. This pleased God so much that God bestowed a large blessing of wealth and prosperity on Solomon as well as the Spirit of Wisdom he asked for. Solomons example here is a key to success.

When you sincerely want to be a help and be a blessing to others that you serve, this pleases God and He will bless you with wealth and prosperity as well. If you are seeking wealth and prosperity, that is not the abundance you will receive. You must be unselfish and have a heart to give and govern wisely those under your umbrella.

People tend to want to pick and choose who they help, who they serve, and who they give to. This is not a wise thing to do. You must listen to the voice of the Holy Spirit and give to and serve who God wants you to, even if it's something about them you do not like. Blessings are held up because of this type of selfishness.

Even in a marriage, if your spouse is not doing what you feel they should be doing, you are commanded to still do right by the other spouse. There is a blessing for your obedience.

Not one person is perfect. I can't stress that enough. Everyone has a thorn. "...even though I have received wonderful revelations from God. But to keep me from getting puffed up, I was given a thorn in my flesh, a messenger from Satan to torment me and keep me from getting proud." 2Corinthians 12:7 NLT.

It is clear two of Solomons thorns were alcohol and women and his wise mother tried to help him with that. What we see here is a direct message from the Lord: God's Chosen people are not perfect people. God uses you and blesses you with your thorns in active mode out of your obedience to your calling.

Solomon, with all his wisdom and riches, knew that material gain meant nothing in contrast to your dying soul because of your sinful nature.

God gives Grace to his Chosen for their thorns. Solomon had a brother killed to be sure he became King, and God still blessed him to be the wisest and wealthiest man of his era. Over and over in the Bible we see the Chosen men and women of God being imperfect people, just like us today.

You must give Grace and understanding for the thorns of your spouse, to effectively travel the journey as a Power Couple. "There is no condemnation in Christ Jesus." God is for and with us all, despite the thorns, and you need to be understanding of this also.

Chosen does not mean perfect. Chosen means imperfectly leaning on the Lord.

36

CHAPTER 36

SINGLE PEPS - ALWAYS WANT GOD'S WILL

I sincerely believe our dreams and aspirations are placed within us by the Holy Spirit. The drive to pursue your purpose is the motivation behind knowing what you were created to do.

You know what you were created to do because the Holy Spirit placed His will within you and your desire to accomplish that purpose lines up with the Will of God for you to do so. God said in Jeremiah 29:11 that He knows the plans he has for you. You didn't come up with those plans. God placed them within you and when you are in His will, you have a desire to fulfill them.

God also says in several verses that He will give you the desires of your heart. If you delight yourself in the Lord, if you put your trust in Him, He will act. John 15:7 says if you abide in me, and my words abide in you, ask whatever you wish, and it will be done for you. The word of God that abides in you is His desire for your life. You're abiding in Him is you being obedient to His will, and by doing so, His will for you becomes your will for yourself. Once you know what your will for yourself is, just ask God to execute it and He will, because it's what He wants for and from you anyway. Your will for yourself is now exactly what God's will be for you.

There are steps to getting the desires of your heart. There are requirements on your end for the Kingdom of Heaven, and in return you will be blessed with your desires. These desires did not just appear out of your own mind, these desires were placed within you by the Holy Spirit. These desires are what's best for you, they are what you need to continue your spiritual journey, and they align with what God will bless you with. You only need to earn them, so to speak. You earn them by being obedient to the word of God.

I believe this to be true when it comes to your mate. That picture that you have in your mind of who your mate should be, was not placed there by you. All the steps of God's Chosen Vessel are ordered from above. Including the mate, he has designed for you or designed you for. Just like he created Eve to be everything Adam could ever need or want in a wife.

Mistakes happen in a marriage, just like with Adam and Eve. But that doesn't mean you are supposed to leave the marriage. It means accepting the consequences and learning from them alongside your mate and continuing in your union for a lifetime.

What too many of us do when we become impatient waiting on God to send the true mate for us, we compromise what we want and accept something less than what God has for us. This brings disaster and turmoil to our marriage and most times the Chosen vessel is unable to walk in their Divine Destiny. This is the trick of the enemy.

Do not listen to people who tell you to lower your standards when it comes to your mate. That's the enemy trying to trick you and keep you from your blessing. The desire you have for a particular mate was placed in you by God. It's what God is saying you need, and He will supply just that in due season.

Mathew 21:22 says, "Whatever you ask in prayer, you will receive, if you have faith." That is what is expected of you. Pray and have faith and you will receive the mate that you envision yourself with.

I suggest you write out every single detail of the mate you want. Pray and ask God what characteristics the mate for you has, and He will tell you. What height, what shape, what eating habits, what profession, if you desire to be a Power Couple write that as well and what it will look like in your marriage. Write it all down and present the final desires to God.

Watch God do it!

37

CHAPTER 37

WHY WE NEED PEOPLE

For so many of my adult years I would feel as though I didn't need people. All I needed was God and that was it. I became introverted, isolating myself, and I would say to others, "I don't need friends, I have a friend in Jesus". This came from a place of hurt. What I learned was, who you associate with and allow to be an active part of your life will make or break you. *But do not fret because what's broken can be fixed.*

After working on my self-healing journey, I realized that I do have a friend in Jesus, but I need tangible people in my life as well. The important key is "what kind of people" I need in my life.

Since my healing journey began, I have been gaining new relationships and meeting people I know are my true friends, and the love from my family and current friends has seemed to increase. Every tear I cried in isolation is being replaced with a ray of love to overshadow any hurt, any doubt, and my pain.

My gratitude level is tipping the scales because I haven't lost or walked away from, but only gained and walked into. Nothing I have experienced has been in vain. Everything has had a significant purpose. What seemed ugly, turned beautiful. What was bad and painful, God turned into good and comfortable. The greatest increase has been the gaining of new relationships.

I don't think I need a whole lot of people in my close circle, but I do need close friends and some associates in my life. I isolated myself for many years because of traumas and hurt from some of the people I associated with. I thought the remedy to further avoid that type of pain was to not have friends and I wouldn't get hurt. However, I still would end up hurt by close family members or my spouse, and I realized experiencing some level of disappointment and hurt in relationships cannot be avoided. It's how we develop and grow in this area.

I began to study the betrayal of God's Chosen by close friends, spouses, and family members in the Bible. This type of hurt is common all throughout the Bible, even Jesus was betrayed and lied to by close friends and associates. I realized it is a part of life and separating yourself from "people", family included, will not stop you from experiencing the ups, downs, joys, and pains, that come from the needed relationships with "people". In fact, it is a necessary part of growth in our lives.

How you handle the unpleasantness that may arise with someone is what will make the difference. We must be wise in how we handle our relationships with others. Depending on what the relationship is will determine the best way to handle it, but isolation is not the answer. In fact, I will go so far as to say, isolation is a trick of the enemy and will prevent you from walking in your purpose.

People and family members who you know genuinely love you, do yourself a favor and allow them space in your life. No one is perfect and accepting people for who they are is a sign of maturity. A lot of times we cut off family members and close friends that love us and will pray for us because we don't like something they did in the past or we don't like a part of their personality. Understand that we all have imperfections, and exercising forgiveness is vital in relationships and will take you far in your life. Having those prayers in your favor is needed.

"Faithful are the wounds of a friend, but deceitful are the kisses of an enemy." Proverbs 27:6.

The people who you know that mean you no good, leave them be. If they are practicing habits or living a lifestyle that is opposite of the direction you are going in, love them from a distance. Don't isolate yourself, just don't have them as close associations. The reason you don't isolate yourself from them totally is so your lifestyle as a Christian can be a silent testimony to them of the love of the Lord. Their hearts can be changed in this way.

The enemy will try to place people in your life for the purpose of being a stumbling block to you. If a person in your circle is not able to elevate you in any way, if they are not already where you are trying to be, having them in close association may be a huge hinderance to walking in your purpose. Isolating yourself from them or disassociating yourself abruptly with them may very well cause them to have unpleasant thoughts and feelings towards you, which will negatively affect you in some way. You want to have a good name for yourself and be a pleasant memory with everyone as much as you possibly can. This will get you far and prevent demonic attacks that arise from discord, hatred, anger, malice, and jealousy from other people.

In extreme cases where a relationship or friendship must be severed, try to do so without terminating the relationship in a hurtful way. Always apologize and be forgiving. Never be rude or revengeful.

For example, if you have decided to stop getting high or stop drinking and that is what those who you associate with are doing, it may be necessary for you to sever the friendship and create a peaceful distance. Set strong boundaries and don't give in to the temptations of returning to those behaviors. In this case become an example and be close enough to where they can witness your change, but distant enough to where you cannot be drawn back in.

If the relationship is one of adultery or similar, you need to sever the relationship and the communication on a peaceful note.

It is healthy to have good friends. Good friends will support your vision, be there for you when the going gets tough, and give you companionship to keep lonely days away. Getting together and laughing with good friends will warm your heart and plant memorable moments within you. This will reduce stress in your life.

Associating with people who are where you are trying to go will give you the information you need to accomplish your goals and will boost your confidence and self-esteem.

If you isolate yourself, you will not be able to make these friendships. You must go to where people who have similar interests to yours gather and be open to being social and taking the initiative to create new friendships. This is how you meet those that God will place in your life to help you reach your goals and aspirations.

Smile often and be friendly always. Be a loyal and true trustworthy friend to others. "A man who has friends must himself be friendly..." Proverbs 18:24.

Develop a genuine "love" for your friends. I tell my friends I love them because I do. *Love is an important key ingredient for success in this life.* It's important to have love for the people that support you. It's important to have love for your friends and family. The Bible gives us that key by telling us to "love they neighbor" and "treat others as you want to be treated" which is also showing love. It sounds easy but it's not a lot of genuine love in this world. So many people are selfish and are opportunists that prey on the Chosen with a fake form of love. To recognize this form of fake love in a person, you must try the spirit of the person by the Spirit of God. If their lifestyle and their way of showing love is in line with the Word of God, then you are good, if not, beware and end the close association immediately to avoid getting hurt. As you mature in the Word of God your spirit of discernment will get stronger and you will be able to tell the difference between good intentions and evil intentions. Hebrews 5:13-14 explains this. Maturing in the Word of God is the only way to exercise growing in this area. Another key to a wealthy weapon that a Chosen vessel needs.

Have you ever been to a concert or seen an awards show, and the artist tells their fans that they love them? A successful artist knows that genuine love for their supporters sends more love back to them. Love begets love, and that type of genuine love comes with benefits. Benefits equal wealth. That artist is who he is today because of the love of his fans, by him showing more love back, his fan base is increased and that's money in his bank. Keep in mind this is a *genuine love* coming from the artist, and it can be felt by his audience and fans.

This type of genuine love is across the board though, it's not a love that is directed towards one sector of people. You must have a heart of love for **all**. Which means you love your enemies as well as your friends. **This is where most people fail**. But the few who understand this concept and have filled their hearts with love for all creation are reaping the wealthiest benefits. The reason why they love their enemies is because their haters push them to strive for greater elevation within their accomplishments. And for this they are thankful. Loving your enemies is a key component to success, the Bible clearly states with the red words of Jesus, **"But to you who are listening I say: Love your enemies, do good to those who hate you, pray for those who mistreat you."** Luke 6:27-28.

38

CHAPTER 38

DARK FORCES/HOW WE FIGHT

As a Chosen vessel you can love your enemies and be thankful for their existence because you know these four things God has promised you: 1. God fights your battles and avenges your enemies, 2. No weapon formed against you will prosper, 3. All things will work out in your favor, and 4. The evil meant against you will be used for your good.

In the book of Genesis, we find the story of Joseph. So much evil was done to him, and he did suffer pain and hurt as a result, especially since it was his own brothers that intended to bring harm upon him. But in the end God turned all those evil intentions done to him into steppingstones that lead to his esteemed position which gave him authority over many, including those who had evil intentions for him. In Genesis 50:20, Joseph says something that lets us know this is how God works for his Chosen. He says to his brothers, "But as for you, you meant evil against me; but God meant it for good, in order to bring it about as it is this day, to save many people alive."

This is a clear example of how the evil intentions of your enemies are necessary to catapult you into your Divine Destiny. A person can be your loving friend today and an enemy tomorrow and a person can be your enemy today and your loving friend tomorrow. You are created strong enough to handle evil attacks against you, and wise enough to know that in the end it is for the greater good of your ministry. This is why you pray for your enemies' well-being and salvation and treat them the way you would want to be treated in love. Be thankful for their presence in your life because their evil intentions against you have pushed you to even greater greatness.

Since God is fighting your battles on your behalf, you are to pray to Him about your concerns regarding your enemies. Everything that happens in your life, God has the knowledge of and has permitted. Satan may be the one directly instigating the attacks against you, but he did so with the permission of God. We know this from the book of Job 1:6-12.

1. Satan does not know the outcome of his attacks against you, if he did, he wouldn't try certain things that only propel you to higher greatness. 2. Satan can only do what God allows him to do against you. 3. You're praying to God about the attacks of your enemies gives you strength to not break under pressure, and 4. You then overcome demonic attacks through the power of God.

In Luke 22:31 we see that Satan directly asked God to attack Peter. Jesus was aware of this, and He prayed for Peter, knowing Peter would fall, but would get back up and become a powerful man of God and leader.

In 2 Corinthians 12:7, Paul admits that his thorn in his flesh was given to him by a messenger of Satan to harass him and keep him from being excessively exalted.

Three times Paul cried out to God and begged God to allow this demonic influential attack to depart from him, and God said to Paul, "My grace, which is My favor and My loving kindness and My mercy, is enough for you, (sufficient against any danger and enables you to bear the trouble manfully), for My strength and power are made perfect, meaning it is fulfilled and completed, and show themselves most effective in your weakness."

This is the battle of good and evil, you who are Chosen must be content with the path you must walk and stay humbly in communication/prayer with the One who fights your battles and gives you strength. The battle will then be won.

How you fight the battle is a key to success because with each battle won you are catapulted towards greater heights. Ephesians 6: 10-18 tells you exactly how to fight your battles with the entire armor of God. Not part...but the full and entire armor of God. Part won't do the job and operating in only part of the armor of God will hold you back from getting to your destiny. The importance of using the entire armor of God cannot be overly stressed.

Modified for your understanding: Ephesians 6:10-18

10. The Holy Spirit dwells within you and gives you immeasurable power. Allow this knowledge to give you the strength you need to always stand and draw from that strength whenever needed.

11. God gives you the armor that is equivalent to that of a heavily armed soldier, put that full armor on, that you will be able to successfully stand up against all the attacks and deceits of the enemy.

12. Your opponents are not human contenders; humans are only vessels that are being used. Your true opponents are the evil rulers and evil powers that are spiritual forces in the darkness and reside in heavenly places or the spiritual realm of this world.

13. This is why you need the full armor of God to withstand such forces, because you are only human yourself and you cannot withstand a battle with a spiritual being without the aid of another spiritual being, which in your case is the Holy Spirit. With this spiritual armor you will be able to stand firm when crisis and dangers attack you.

Here is the Armor of God that you need:

14. You must know the Word of God so you can stand on God's Word when Satan comes at you with lies. The Spirit of Truth prevails over the spirit of lies. Satan fights with lies and he is crafty enough to make his lies sound like truth. The Spirit of Truth placed in you through God's Word will recognize the lies of the enemy and defeat him with truth. This is your Spiritual Belt. Your Spiritual Breastplate is your righteousness which is walking in integrity and having Godly morals and Godly standards.

15. Your Spiritual Footgear is your preparation of the Gospel of Peace, meaning you talking to others about the goodness of God and bringing others to a new life in Christ. Satan will tell you it is worthless and useless to talk

to anyone about how good God has been to you. The Spiritual Footgear from the Holy Spirit gives you the motivation and encouragement you need to win souls for Christ. In Christ we have a peace that surpasses all understanding, and we need to share that with lost souls. Philippians 4:7.

16. Your Spiritual Shield is your faith. This Shield of Faith protects you from the fiery darts of the enemy. We are attacked in the form of insults, scandalizing of our name, setbacks, and temptations. With the Shield of Faith, you know regardless of how the situation may look in the natural world, you win in the end.

17. Your Spiritual Helmet is the assurance of your Salvation in a dying world. This is a direct attack against your mind. Your thoughts will be attacked by the enemy. This is why you take every thought captive. 2 Corinthians 10:5, "Casting down arguments and every high thing that exalts itself against the knowledge of God, bringing every thought into captivity to the obedience of Christ." When you realize your thoughts are not lining up with the Word of God, or you start to doubt what God has told you is true, with the Spiritual Helmet you will recognize this is the enemy and cast down those thoughts and take them into captivity. Lock them up and throw away the key! Salvation is yours and you are free. Saved from the pits of hell by the Grace of God. Press on Soldier.

18. Your Spiritual Sword is Prayer, and you must pray without ceasing. 1 Thessalonians 5:16. Never stop praying. James 5:16 declares "the effectual, fervent, continued prayer of a righteous man makes tremendous power available". Pray every day, every season, every occasion, before you eat, before you sleep, when you wake up, and every free moment that you have. Be watchful and mindful of any and everything you need to pray about in your life and in the life of other believers. Prayer is a very powerful weapon.

Mathew 6:6 tells us we will be rewarded openly for praying private sincere prayers. That's a key to success.

Always remember me when you pray and pray for me as well. Pray for my children and my grandchildren if I'm no longer living on Earth.

As long as you are operating in your full armor, the bottom line is this right here: "We are pressed on every side by troubles, but we are not crushed and broken. We are perplexed, but we don't give up and quit. We are hunted down, but God never abandons us. We get knocked down, but we get up again and keep going." 2 Corinthians 4:8-9.

39

CHAPTER 39

TAKING THE KINGDOM BY FORCE

overall

"For He will give His angels especial charge over you to accompany and defend and preserve you in all your ways of obedience and service". Psalms 91:11.

Hell also has levels, but the important thing to know is that Satan does not currently dwell in hell. Satan roams the earth for the sole purpose of tempting people to live in sin and separate them from God when they do so. 1 Peter 5:8, "Be alert and of sober mind. Your enemy the devil prowls around like a roaring lion looking for someone to devour".

Jesus said in John 14:30, Satan is the "prince of this world". We have only two master's that we can choose to serve and it's God in Heaven or Satan. The King of kings or the prince of darkness. If you aren't serving God, then you are serving Satan.

Satan has access to earth and heavenly places. Ephesians 6:12 tell us this. Job 2:1-2 says, "On another day the angels came to present themselves before the LORD, and Satan also came with them to present himself. And the LORD said to Satan, 'Where have you come from?' Satan answered the LORD, 'From roaming through the earth and going back and forth in it.'

There is a spiritual battle that takes place in heavenly places. The spiritual battle we fight in the natural here on earth does not include contact weaponry or physical warfare because the battle is one of spiritual nature on our end. The entire war takes place in heavenly places.

"From the days of John, the Baptist until now the kingdom of heaven suffers violence, and violent men take it by force." Mathew 11:12.

The proposed question is: If the Kingdom of Heaven suffers violence, and the violent are taking it by force, who is fighting violently if it's not us, or is it?

The proposed answer is: Being that the Kingdom of Heaven belongs to God and those on the Lord's side, and the Kingdom of Heaven is being taken, then those who are on the Lord's side are fighting violently and taking it by force.

Those on the Lord's side fight on earth and in heavenly places. This makes up the army of the Lord. We are soldiers on the battlefield for the Lord. We must fight in this world to get the blessings of God which are promised to us because dark and evil forces are trying to keep us from it. These evil forces are trying to take our life. The way Chosen vessels fight this spiritual battle is of a spiritual nature. As you have learned, you need to have on your full armor.

Psalm 91:11 – He has put his angels on charge of you to watch over you wherever you go.

The Chosen are protected. We have strong angelic forces in Heavenly places that fight on our behalf. Where Satan can go, our angelic protectors can go as well. When angels appeared to people in the Bible, their presence was so majestic that the Bible says the people would be afraid and terrified. These are our spiritual bodyguards. Our prayers activate the movement of our spiritual guardians on our behalf, and they fight against the dark powers violently for us. When we cry out to God to move on our behalf because we are being attacked by the enemy, He sends angelic forces to overpower the demonic forces that are attacking us. Your fervent prayers and your effectual purpose are the motivation needed as ammunition to win your battles.

Now peep this, the prayers of the wicked do the very same thing on the opposing team. There are people who walk this earth that worship dark forces and use their gifts for a satanic army. They are against the Kingdom of God. They come after the heirs of God's Kingdom with a vengeance and their prayers against the Chosen activate a spiritual fight to destroy their target.

They pray to the forces of darkness for your demise. The same way we pray to God, is the same way they pray to Satan. Then begins a spiritual warfare. The demonic beings and the angelic beings began to battle in heavenly places.

Our bodies feel the evidence of spiritual warfare. We are tired and drained, sometimes weary, and doubtful from the fight we are facing. The key is to not stop praying, praising, and believing for your victory to be won, and the angels that fight for you will win that battle just like promised! Faith is your shield.

Too often many give up the fight just before their breakthrough. In those times that you feel as though God is not answering and you will lose the battle, you need to fight the hardest for what you are believing God for. Pray violently without ceasing and keep your blessing from the enemy by force.

The Kingdom of Heaven belongs to God and no demonic forces will be able to conquer it. We are Chosen, we are strong victors, we have a track record of overcoming, we don't give up, and we fight violently for what we know is ours with the help of angelic warriors.

40

CHAPTER 40

LOSING/CHANGING THE COMPANY YOU KEEP

Your associations directly affect your level. I can look at your associations and see where you are in your life. Eagles can't fly with ravens because the ravens cannot reach the designed heights of eagles. Hanging with ravens will keep you from soaring as an eagle should. Eagles soar with other eagles.

Jesus and his immediate circle were all wealthy businessmen, entrepreneurs, and tax collectors. Jesus had lucrative investors, sponsorship, and was always receiving expensive gifts, oils, gold, money, etc. And these were the people he hung around and allowed to be in his personal space. There is a reason for that, and it is one that we should learn from.

Being friendly and making friendships with high vibrational people plays a big role in accomplishing your goals. The biggest reason is because it is contagious. By adopting the habits of wealthy and high vibrational people, you will start learning how to create and maintain wealth, which will continue to attract others who are wealthy and high vibrational to you. These types of relationships will motivate you and lift you up, as opposed to associating with those who will bring you down or leave you stagnant because of the lack of motivation to excel.

You want to have people who are where you are striving to be in your life, not just monetarily but spiritually, socially, and mentally, any others are only distractions. Avoid and discontinue relationships with people who have bad habits, no goals, negative disposition, oppressed mentality, no gratitude, little faith, dishonesty, and immature thought patterns and actions. Instead, befriend people who are trustworthy, disciplined, have high morals and healthy boundaries, strong faith, financially stable, compassion for others, goal oriented, positive mindset, good habits, willing to help and advise you, honest, and generally happy.

"The righteous choose their friends carefully, but the way of the wicked leads them astray." Proverbs 12:26.

When it comes to friendships, they should be built with those whose choose to live God's way, any other way is the way of darkness. These types of friends will encourage you to go the path God has designed for you to live when you want to go astray as well. You need that in your life because you will continue to be tempted to abort the path of righteousness. Which always leads to destruction, and you don't want that for yourself.

You can't tell your dreams and aspirations to others, even family. Many wealthy people will have new friendships and business relationships sign an NDA, which is a legal contract that requires parties to keep certain information confidential and not disclose it to others without permission. Don't be offended by this at all. Instead, learn from this and adopt the same standards when necessary. If you encounter someone who refuses to sign such an agreement to confidentiality, then this is someone you cannot trust.

Anyone who does not understand or believe in your vision should not be in your life. Do not associate with people who are not visionaries themselves. The people in your life should have a positive purpose to be a part of your life. The purpose should somehow be to help you towards your vision, even if it is just to give you encouragement. Before opening the door for someone to be in your life, identify what the purpose is for them to be a part of your circle. Know and understand that God will place people in your life to help you succeed.

Ask yourself these questions concerning those in your life or new associations:

1. Does my association with this person help me better myself?
2. Does this person have information I don't have and need? Are they willing to share this information?
3. Will this person drain me of my time? Money? Joy? Peace?

If the person adds no value to your life, there is no need for you to associate with them. When you realize a person that is in your life no longer adds value to your life, their season as an associate or friend has expired and needs to be terminated. People will drain you dry if you allow them to, instead of being a service and inspiration to you.

Sexual relations with low vibrational people will also have a negative effect on you if you are functioning on a higher vibration. If you are pursuing your goals and you are operating on a high vibrational frequency, and you hook up just for sex with someone who has low vibrational energy, you're putting yourself at great risk because you are opening yourself up to spirits that will bring your spirit and vibration level down. Because remember whatever is inside of them will be transferred inside of you during intercourse. You don't want to take this risk because it will set your energy at a lower frequency, and you can't accomplish the things that you have to accomplish being on a low vibrational frequency level. This is how people bring you down without you even realizing that you've been brought down until it is too late. And you may not even realize where the setback came from. This is a service that will cause more damage than good in the long run. You may feel the temporary sexual gratification is meeting a need, but it is a trick of the enemy to find his way into your housing and bring negativity into your thought process.

Operating in the Anointing leaves your spirit man weary and tired. Coming within the presence of the Holy Spirit leaves you drained, and you will have to be spiritually restored and rested to get your energy level back up. Dealing with people who will drain you and weigh down your spirit is just too much to add to that equation. It is to your benefit to end relationships that do not serve you in a positive compacity.

41

CHAPTER 41

HOW JESUS DEALT WITH TOXIC PEOPLE

One day the Pharisees and scribes brought a woman to Jesus who had been caught in the act of adultery. They said to Jesus that Mose's law commands the woman be stoned to death and asked him what he says they should do with her. These dudes were always testing Jesus and trying to trap him in a lie, but Jesus was not going to fall for it, ever. Jesus stooped down and started writing in the sand. Ignoring them, but they persisted and continued to question Jesus. He finally got up and simply said "Let him who is without sin amongst you be the first to throw a stone at her." And then he bent down and went back to writing in the sand with his finger. No one could touch that answer so they just all slowly left until no one was left in the center of the court but Jesus and the woman. Jesus then looked at the woman and asked her where were her accusers? Is anyone here condemning you? And she answered him, No one, Lord! And Jesus told her to go on her way and don't sin anymore.

Jesus did not argue or dispute anything with anyone. In fact, Jesus didn't have long conversations with toxic people. He was short and to the point. He did not engage with them on their own toxic terms. He would even ignore them at times. He would walk away from them or send them away from Him.

This was how Jesus handled toxic people. The adulterous woman was toxic as well and Jesus was short with her and quickly sent her on her way with his advice to not sin anymore.

As Christians we do not need to debate or go back and forth with toxic people. Even if we feel this is being done in love, it is not the example Jesus left for us to follow. It will only cause more problems and make room for the non-believers to find fault with the debating Christian and reflect that one person's behavior on all Christians across the board.

It's useless to debate, argue, or defend yourself or your Christianity. There will be non-believers that will co-exist on Earth with believers and that's life. Allow your lifestyle to minister to them instead. Anything else will appear as if you are not showing love and will only push non-believers further away from becoming a believer. You must draw people with love and kindness. Debating, defending, and arguing does not show any form of love or kindness.

People are going to talk about you and will slander your name. People will ridicule your walk with Christ and your purpose. There's and old saying that says, "They talked about Jesus Christ so what makes you think they won't talk about you too?" That is straight truth. You are not to deem yourself higher than Christ, so humble yourself and let it go.

When the two disciples in Jesus' circle became toxic, he called them out on how they would betray him. They had a clear purpose to be in his circle and when that season was up, he let them know that he knew their disloyalty to betray him. Sometimes we have people in our circle that have a good purpose in our lives and later their loyalty may turn on us and they become toxic to our wellbeing. Judas was his treasurer, and when the time came in Jesus' ministry that Judas's season as treasurer was up and he would betray Jesus's loyalty, Jesus told Judas exactly how he was going to betray him and to go do it quickly. Judas hung himself after he betrayed Jesus. The Bible says Satan entered and took possession of Judas, before he ran out to betray Jesus, and Satan comes to kill, steal, and destroy. Peter was told by Jesus that he would deny his close friendship and association with Jesus three times, and Peter denied to Jesus that he would ever betray him, but he did just that. The Bible states that when Peter denied Jesus the third time, he invoked a curse upon himself. We must be very careful of the words that we say, and that we are not bringing curses upon ourselves. Most often silence is golden. Peter was later killed by hanging upside down.

When someone in your circle that once was a good asset to you becomes a burden or no longer serves you in a positive way, you can gently let them know why it's best to part ways and quietly do so. No need to gossip or make a big stink about it, just be short and kind in how you address them and request their absence from your close association moving forward. If their betrayal has shocked and hurt you, leave that to God to revenge on your behalf. I'm sure it grieved Jesus's heart to know his best buddies and business partners would betray him because he called Judas "friend" during the betrayal kiss, and when Jesus was seized all his disciples ran and left him. Yet he had to continue his purpose and mission for a higher cause.

When Jesus was seized, he was tied up and bound. Peter who was the quick tempered one that would draw his sword and cut off someone's ear for coming incorrect to Jesus, had betrayed him and was not around, and all the other disciples fled and left him. People took this opportunity to spit on Jesus and physically slap and hit him. This was assault and a jailable offense that they got away with. I'm more than positive many of these people were in the crowds that Jesus spoke to and taught. That's how people are, they will kick you when you are down and cannot defend yourself. Even those you have poured into and helped in some kind of way. Those that you think would be in your corner, will not, and those you think would never harm you, will.

Jesus remained quiet during most of this unless he was provoked tirelessly to respond. When he did respond to their absorbed questions and allegations, it was short and non-accusatory. When people you care about and love hurt you, it's better to stay quiet because if your love wasn't enough, your words won't make a difference.

Again, these things happened to Jesus Christ, and they will surely happen to you. Follow the example of Jesus in how to handle such situations and you will keep down confusion.

42

CHAPTER 42

NARCISSISM = LOVE BOMBING, GASLIGHTING, ENTITLEMENT, OPPORTUNIST...

Man finds a label for everything and tags it as such. The way people behave today is not new. The Bible is filled with stories of people during biblical times with the same characteristics of narcissists today. The pain they caused to others then is just as great as the pain narcissists put people through today.

"What has been will be again, what has been done will be done again; there is nothing new under the sun." Ecclesiastes 1:9.

People who have certain mannerisms and characteristics need to be avoided and deleted from your life. It is for your greater good to do so. They are not where you are spiritually and mentally and that is damaging to your spirit and mental wellbeing. And if you are a person that has some of these traits and/or characteristics, do yourself justice and work hard right away to change them, so you aren't the person being deleted from someone's life.

Opportunists are people who see a chance to gain some advantage from a situation, often at the expense of someone else and their own ethics or morals. Their main thought pattern is, "What can I get from this?"

These types of people know exactly how and where to benefit from other people's personal gains, kindness, and giving. They will do all they can to get the most out of it, so they don't miss out on anything. The fastest way to get it is the approach they will take. Leeching off someone else is the #1 goal for opportunists.

Opportunists will love bomb and smooth talk their way into your life so you can open up to them and they can suck you dry for what they can get out of you. Love bombing is attempts to influence another person with over-the-top praises, displays of affection, and attention. Your judgement is hopefully weakened by this so they can take advantage of you. If you see this coming and call them out on it, they will insult you and try to make you feel guilty and ashamed as if you are the bad person for calling them out.

A lot of men prey on women who seem vulnerable and are seeking for companionship. They do not want to be providers in the household as they should be. Beware of these behaviors of the opportunist. The only way a King can rule over a Kingdom is to own it. The only way he can own it, is to have purchased it with his own blood, sweat, and tears.

True relationships will have a balance of giving and taking. An opportunist is a taker and if they do give, it is very small in comparison to what you are giving to them. You will be the one who normally foots the bill, and the truth is they have little or no interest in how their actions are affecting you.

Some opportunists will want to befriend you to associate with other people in your circle and you know nothing about the people they associate with.

Healthy relationships develop naturally and with no ulterior motives. Both parties give to the other and help one another genuinely. There is no price tag or obligation for their friendship.

Opportunists will want to get close to you because of what they believe you can do for them and once they get what they want, they will exit and leave you in some form of despair. Most opportunists will also classify as narcissists.

Narcissism is a term that encompasses many personality traits which include a sense of entitlement. The entitlement thinking pattern is defined as a sense of deservingness or special treatment towards something they did not earn or purchase. An example of entitlement is a person coming into your home and feeling or behaving as though what you have belongs to them as well, simply because they are there. Do not tolerate such foolishness.

The narcissist can be overt or covert. The major difference between both types of narcissists is that overt narcissists are open about their arrogant, delusional, selfish, and self-absorbing personalities. But the covert narcissists tend to hide theirs and portray more humane qualities to obtain favor and fool others. The covert narcissist is less obvious and may come across as shy, withdrawn, introverted, and self-depreciating. The overt narcissist is extroverted, attention seeking, and aggressive or violent if their sense of status is challenged.

The overt narcissist is more obvious, and you can better spot them and protect yourself. The covert narcissist is more passive in their control and manipulation. The overt is open with their narcissistic qualities and the covert hides them. The covert narcissist can be more difficult to spot because they aren't loud and, in your face. This might make them worse than the overt narcissist in some cases.

Both types of narcissists have an inflated sense of self and have no empathy for others. Narcissists tend to project blame on others and gaslight. Gaslighting is the act of repeatedly lying to someone to manipulate, and ultimately control them and the relationship. It includes outright lying, manipulation of reality, scapegoating, and coercion. Gaslighting and manipulation is a form of emotional and psychological abuse.

The narcissist has an agenda to win, dominate, and get what they want at the expense of the other person's wellbeing. They will play with other people's lives as if it is merely a game. Their behaviors are very toxic, and they will shift the blame, deflect, and attack. They will look for people who will side with them and tell them that you are wrong and evil, and they are right and good. It involves lying, smearing, slandering, triangulating, gossiping, stalking, and other forms of social aggression and manipulation. They will tell other people that you are the one that behaves in a mentally unstable manner and call you crazy. You are only crazy to people who cannot manipulate and control you.

Winning to a narcissist is dominating, bullying, deceiving, demeaning, humiliating, and hurting others. They look at every situation as a win-lose opportunity. Narcissists do not form emotional attachments and don't care how they beat you at their game and will take no shame in tearing you apart shred by shred. In fact, this may even be their motive.

It is useless to engage in any way with anyone who uses these types of tactics. These types of people are not interested in your view, your thoughts, or how you feel. They don't care about solutions or compromises. Even if they say they care about it, their actions will prove that they do not.

Try not to respond to a narcissist with defense or empathy. They have neither towards you; it will only fuel them further. Please make a keynote that Jesus did not respond to toxic people with emotion and Jesus did not respond to them with empathy either.

It is best to have no contact with people like this and cease communication. By removing yourself from their game this will change their desired outcome, and it will remove any power they may hold over you.

Beware of the bait and withdraw tactic of the narcissist. The covert narcissist, more so than the overt, is notorious for ghosting and abandoning their targeted prey after a bond has been formed. Once you have been ghosted or abandoned and they feel you may be slipping out of their threshold and moving closer to becoming unattached and trauma bonded with them, they will reappear to bait you back in and give you just enough attention filled with lies and promises they do not intentionally plan to keep, and then they will withdraw by ghosting and abandoning you again. This is to take you back to your previous state of brokenness and to reopen the wound that was close to being healed from the trauma they caused you, because in this broken state they have control over you and your attention is focused on them again, as you blindly are remaining in a state of longing for them to be present with you. This feeds their false sense of superiority and dominance over you. This power has them believing they are in a winning position.

Do not allow these types of people back into your life once you have escaped their grip. They have proven that their behaviors towards you are not loving and are abusive emotionally and/or physically. Do not trust that they have changed. They do not deserve to be in your space again. If you insist to allow them back into your life, then the two of you should have therapy together, and you should not move forward unless a licensed professional feel it is safe for this person to be in your life. Even then get to know them all over again much slower than you did before. Pray and ask God is this someone that should be in your life after God removed/saved you from that traumatic situation in the first place.

A person that is unholy and has no fear of God will have no regard for you who are Chosen. This makes them dangerous because they run after their own lusts and will not stop at nothing to take what they feel they should have, destroying whoever gets in their way or tries to correct them. You, Chosen, are a gift from God and these types of people set out to destroy the gifts from God like a child destroys their toys. I have found that these types of people do not change without an act of God forcing them to acknowledge God like God did to King Nebuchadnezzar.

King Nebuchadnezzar was a narcissist in the Bible. This King thought himself to be so powerful that he thought he was more powerful than God! He was so evil with narcissism that God took his power away and forced him to go away from people and live as a wild animal and eat grass like an ox. Seven years he lived as though he was insane in the wilderness until he humbled himself and acknowledge God. Nebuchadnezzar tells this story himself in the book of Daniel 4.

This is why you are instructed to leave narcissistic people alone. Have absolutely nothing to do with them because you cannot help them, and they will drain you dry if you try. People, including mates and potential mates, are investments. You invest your time, money, and emotions in people. It is a key to wealth building to invest these things on fertile ground when it comes to people in our lives as well. Refrain from investing anything in these types of individuals. This is truly a situation where you "let go and let God", and God will handle them as he did Nebuchadnezzar and we know this to be true because His word says that "at the name of Jesus every knee shall bow, of those in heaven, and of those on earth, and of those under the earth, and that every tongue confess that Jesus Christ is Lord, to the Glory of God the Father." Philippians 2:10-11.

The Bible gives us the Characteristics of narcissists in 2 Timothy 3: "1 You should know this, Timothy, (substitute your name for Timothy because this is for you), that in the last days there will be very difficult times. 2 For people will love only themselves and their money. They will be boastful and proud, scoffing at God, disobedient to their parents, and ungrateful. They will consider nothing sacred. 3 They will be unloving and unforgiving; they will slander others and have no self-control. They will be cruel and hate what is good. 4 They will betray their friends, be reckless, be puffed up with pride, and love pleasure rather than God. 5 They will act religious, but they will reject the power that could make them godly. **Stay away from people like that!** 6 They are the kind who work their way into people's homes and win the confidence of vulnerable women who are burdened with the guilt of sin and controlled by various desires (passions). (The Entitled Opportunist Narcissist that I explained to you about!) 7 (Such women are forever following new teachings (always learning), but they are never able to understand the truth.) *I have spelled out the truth to you, please strongly regard what I have shared in this book and know it comes from a place of experience and don't be the woman that is being spoken of here in the Bible.* 8 These teachers oppose the truth just as Jannes and Jambres opposed Moses. They have depraved minds and a counterfeit faith. 9 **But they won't get away with this for long.** Someday everyone will recognize what fools they are, just as with Jannes and Jambres."

Jannes and Jambres are thought to be the two chief magicians who opposed Moses and Aaron when Aaron threw down his staff in front of Pharaoh and it turned into a snake. Pharoah called in the magicians, and they threw down their staff and it became a snake as well. But Aaron's snake swallowed up their snake. Later the same magicians duplicated turning the water into blood and the production of frogs. They were powerless to duplicate the other plagues. This took place in the Old Testament without the mentioning of their names, yet they are being mentioned by name in the New Testament as being recognized as having depraved minds and a counterfeit faith. They too had to recognize what fools they were. They are the example being used to describe how foolish people are that will oppose the Chosen vessels of

God and seek to destroy them and their reputation. God does handle such individuals accordingly.

43

CHAPTER 43

FREE WILL

God in all His awesomeness gives us the freedom to choose. We as humans, have free will. We cannot choose our immediate family, but we can choose who we will marry and reproduce with. We can choose our friends, our occupation, and everything in life is our choice, even who or what we will serve, obey, and pledge our allegiance to.

"Above all else, guard your heart, for it is the wellspring of life." Proverbs 4:23. We guard what is important and special to you, but for some reason we don't realize how important and valuable our hearts are. If we did, then we wouldn't end up in so many hurtful situations.

Your heart being your wellspring of life is letting you know that everything you do, say, and think includes your heart. There is no decision made without your heart being the source of the final decision. If your heart is in a sunken state, it will have a direct impact on your decision-making process.

You must choose wisely in what you do and how you move, guarding your heart while doing so. You don't want to choose toxic situations and place your heart in a toxic environment. Doing so will hold up your legacy building.

Being Chosen has you under constant attack from the enemy. The higher your position and the more sheep you have under your umbrella, the more severe the attacks will be. The enemy is going straight for your heart.

Even situations that leave you disappointed, tricked, lonely, feeling like giving up and discouraged, are a matter of the heart being attacked. Most times it is the choices that we make that open the door to being attacked.

And let me not forget to add that God does not choose our mate or the people in our lives for us. God will either send people, or allow people into our lives, and it is our choice who we decide to open ourselves to and build relationships with.

God will also intervene, halt a situation, or someone's will, from the interceding prayers of others. For example, let's say you are in a domestic violence situation, and your loved ones are praying for you to get out of it because your heart is at such a weakened state that you cannot make the choice to leave for yourself. Therefore, God intervenes and causes the violent spouse to have a hardened heart towards you, and to eventually leave. Allowing you to have the space and time to heal and regain strength. This is how a spiritual battle can change the free will of another's choice. The choice made was not one that guarded the heart and was instead damaging to the Chosen vessel. Divine intervention had to be made.

Not guarding your heart in your choices is very costly.

44

CHAPTER 44

FELLOWSHIPPING WITH THE CHURCH

There is a tremendous blessing when you are planted in a church with great leadership. (And you can't find this blessing if you are church hopping or not in church at all.)

Most people go to church to feel closer to God. The feeling of the Holy Spirit in a place where several believers are gathered can be felt in a very powerful way. However, if you have a relationship with your Heavenly Father, His presence can be felt wherever you are because the Holy Spirit dwells within you.

The church is definitely the starting point for those who are choosing to come to Christ for the first time or to rededicate their lives to Christ. With that being said, there needs to be leaders within the church to carry out various ministries for the lost souls, new believers, and the spiritual growth of all those who attend.

This is one of the main reasons God's Chosen people are necessary and needed in the church, to aid the lost and the sin sick in their spiritual healing and growth.

There are benefits for dedicated members of the church outside of being needed to help others. These benefits equate to wealthy gain. Not necessarily monetary gain, but wealth gain for sure.

Hebrews 10:25 tells us not to forsake the assembling of the saints, as it is the habit of some, but to come together to encourage one another because it strengthens us. Some people feel they don't need to come to church or be a part of a body of believers that meet regularly. It is their choice, but it is not the wise choice of one that is Chosen and walking in their Divine Purpose. If an individual chooses to not serve or congregate amongst a body of believers regularly, they will miss out on wealthy gain that comes from doing so.

Relationships amongst one another within the church are very important. There are ways that the relationship with the leaders of the church can be very beneficial to you. Even though you are a Chosen vessel, you will still fall prey to hard times, and you will still have some type of heartache or burden in your life. With these relationships built with other leaders in your church you will have a direct connection for prayer to help you through adversity and to help you fight your battles.

As a tithing member of a church, I once needed financial help when I fell upon hard times financially with my then husband having a loss of his income. Because I paid my tithes regularly, I was able to go to the pastor and ask for the help I needed and received it. Some churches may not require you to be a regular tithing member and others may. Either way, the relationship is important to have for your benefit. You make deposits and when needed you get a return on your investments of relationship building, presence, and the tithing of your time, talents, and treasure.

In the book of Philemon, Paul tells the story of Onesimus. This story is a great illustration of how knowing and having a relationship with your pastor and leaders of the church can be a key instrument to your success by their own association and hierarchy in the community of leaders outside of your church building.

Onesimus name means useful, profitable, beneficial. (As is the need to fellowship with the members of the church community).

Philemon name means loving in Greek. (Which is what the leaders of the church community should be to others).

Philemon was converted to Christianity by the Apostle Paul, who was now his spiritual leader. Philemon was a wealthy landowner and started a church in his home under the leadership of Paul. Philemon was also a slave owner because slavery was very much prevalent during this biblical time in history.

Onesimus was a house slave that belonged to Philemon. Onesimus stole money from Philemon and ran away from his slave owner.

While Paul and some other leaders with him were arrested and placed on house arrest which meant they could still have visitors and somehow, they met Onesimus. Onesimus confessed his sins of stealing from Philemon years prior and running away from him because he was his slave. Paul explained the forgiveness of Christ to Onesimus but also where he was wrong, and Paul led him to give his life to Christ. Onesimus became so close to Paul as he was discipled by him, that Paul referred to him as his own child.

I'm sure Paul recognized the spiritual gifts and how the Lord wanted to use Onesimus, but Onesimus had to return to Philemon because it was the custom and law that a found runaway slave had to be return to his master and could possibly face death.

Paul explained this to Onesimus, and the time came when Onesimus had to return to Philemon. Onesimus walked 1000 miles with the letter from Paul to Philemon not knowing if his life would be spared or not. He had to have incredible faith in God and faith in Paul's position and relationship with Philemon to do so. At any time, he could have detoured and stayed on the run.

Paul skillfully wrote that letter to Philemon on Onesimus behalf. In the letter Paul asked Philemon to accept Onesimus as a brother in Christ and not as his slave and forgive Onesimus for stealing from him and running away. Paul even offered to pay the recompense owned, if any, by Onesimus. Paul said that he loved Onesimus so much that he didn't want him to leave but he knew he had to return to Philemon, because it was the right thing to do, and Philemon would take him in as a brother and allow Onesimus to be used in the Kingdom of God and not as a slave.

Paul even suggested that maybe this was God ordained for Onesimus to run away from Philemon, and meet Paul, to be disciplined into Christianity, and then return to Philemon to help him build the Kingdom of God. Paul made mention in the letter to Philemon that he is his leader, and the one that converted Philemon to Christianity, and he could order Philemon to receive Onesimus back, but he chose for loves sake to make the appeal to Philemon to voluntarily accept Onesimus instead.

Paul told Philemon that he owed him for all that he had done for him and for him to receive Onesimus as he would him. He also ended the letter saying he felt confident that Philemon would be obedient to Paul's wishes and do even more so than what Paul was asking him to do concerning Onesimus.

It is said that Onesimus became a Bishop and had many leaders and churches under his ministry.

Good, honest, leaders in Christ are respected. When you need help outside of their ministry, they can vouch for you on a very large scale. This is a major key to doors opening for you that you cannot open on your own.

I have seen pastors go to court with their parishioners and have them avoid prison time. These types of interventions take time by building relationships while fellowshipping with the church. They require your presence and participation.

It took me years to realize this key point in the importance of being involved with the church and present while fellowshipping and volunteering. I would go, and participate, but to gain insight and wisdom as to why it is so important took time for me to recognize.

People tend to believe that confessing your sins means to tell God about them. What sense does that make when God already knows them?

We are to confess our sins to one another. The reason why is because it is healing in doing so. No one should condemn you or make you feel bad. Love and understanding should be given when someone openly confesses. When confession openly takes place, it is at that moment that forgiveness is extended in the spiritual realm. What is held in the dark secretly can always be used as a weapon against you. There is mental and spiritual freedom in confessing to one another what we feel we have done wrong.

You are held in bondage spiritually when you live in sin or hold your wrong doings within yourself. To be able to confess to a trusted leader who can pray with you and extend love, you must first build a relationship. It builds character and shows to the church that you are growing spiritually and can be an asset to the Kingdom of God. In return, when you need them, they will be there for you.

Fellowshipping with the church can be fun. Doing group events and church trips and picnics are super fun! You get to enjoy singing along with the choir or worship team during service, which gives you good feelings inside. Music is so healing to me, and Gospel Music stirs up the spirit dwelling inside until its light consumes your heart and wipes away any pain or doubt. Singing and dancing is in our DNA, because our ancestors sang and danced for the Lord.

You learn so much in group bible studies. It is very essential and beneficial to have group bible studies. Here you will gain a wealth of knowledge and wisdom that you may not have gotten on your own. You meet accountability partners, prayer partners, and lifelong friends.

Proverbs 12:25 says, "Anxiety in the heart of a man causes depression, but a good word makes it glad".

People pay hundreds, even thousands of dollars, for counseling and therapy. If you are in the right church, you can pocket those dollars. When the pastor or minister gives the message from the Lord, it should be one that makes your heart so glad that it carries you through the week in a happy place as you continually reflect on it. It's hard to catch everything that is being said and that is why many people take notes and reflect on them later. Church is free therapy.

I have been in therapy and recorded the entire session many times so I can reflect later on what was said to me. So, you know without a doubt I will record the Word being ministered in church on my cell phone! Ain't no shame in my game, it's prophetic therapy and I need to reflect on it and hear it again from time to time.

If you are serious about receiving "thus says the Lord" when the Word is spoken and/or preached during the service, then you will reap the benefits of just being counseled by God, through His messenger.

Let your heart be merry like Proverbs says, from your free therapy while fellowshipping with the church. That's a major wealth building key...just fellowshipping with the church. Let him who has ears to hear; hear.

45

CHAPTER 45

UNDERSTANDING THE COST

1. Salvation is free, but maintaining it comes with a price.
2. Wisdom comes with a price.
3. Favor must be earned.

Maintaining salvation has a large price tag. The first thing that salvation will cost you is life as you know it when living for Christ was not a factor. In order to maintain your salvation, you have to die to your flesh daily. You must tell your fleshy desires "No", I cannot do that anymore. As easy as it sounds, it is so hard to do. Which is why we actively still sin as Christians and must repent and keep leaning on His everlasting arms. Following Jesus Christ will cost you everything to stay saved! It requires total commitment and the willingness to give up all things that are not pleasing to God. You may even have to give up your life for the sake of being a Christian. You don't want to be like Peter and deny Christ when times get tough. Salvation will cost you to sacrifice who you were and become a new person in Christ and then you have to fight to remain there. Christ was the sacrificial lamb that died on the cross so we may be saved from the fiery gates of Hell. That is what Salvation is. Accepting

Salvation is free.

James 1:12 says, "Blessed is the man who endures temptation; for when he has been approved, he will receive the crown of life which the Lord has promised to those who love Him." Which is eternal life with God. Salvation.

Wisdom comes with the price of time and the hard experiences that life brings. The longer you live the wiser you should become. The more obstacles you face and overcome the wiser you will become. Each headache and heartbreak should bring some wisdom as you heal through your pain. Each loss and each failure will painfully teach you something new. Therefore, when you ask God for wisdom just hold on to your seat because you are about to suffer in painful ways. If you want patience, you must endure situations that are generally impatient. If you want discipline and self-control, you will be hit with confrontations that will try you. If you want to be courageous, the very things that you fear you must conquer and master. It's cool though, because although wisdom carries a price tag of pain and suffering, we are going to go through obstacles in life anyway, so get wisdom as you go through. Pay the price because it's worth it. No one is going to follow a dummy.

Proverbs 4:7 says this, "The beginning of wisdom is this: Get wisdom. Though it cost all you have, get understanding."

There is a saying that says "favor ain't fair". I don't believe that any more than I believe "sticks and stones will break your bones, but words will never hurt you". Both are lies in my book.

Words can hurt more than being hit and words can bring years of lifelong trauma because of the mental agony attached to it.

Favor is fair because favor is earned. Anything earned had a cost attached to it. Those who think favor is not fair are jealous of those who have it, but it's no need to be jealous because those who have it put the work in to obtain it. Favor isn't free, it comes with the price tag of obedience. You have to give God your life, your time, your money, your service, your humility, your gifts, your worship, your praise, your honor, your love, your prayer, your conversation, your heart, you must go where He say go, you must go when He say go, you must do what He say do and then some! Everybody is not willing to give God their entire being and then they have the audacity to be jealous of someone else who earned the favor of God. A favored child of God can ask for anything, and they know they will get it because they know they have done what is required to receive it. Along with the faith of the favored, they are confident that nothing will be withheld from them.

2 Chronicles 16:9 says, "For the eyes of the Lord run to and fro throughout the whole earth, to show Himself strong on behalf of those whose heart is loyal to Him". God looks for those who are obedient and gives their entire being to Him so He can pour His favor upon them.

46

CHAPTER 46

TAMING THE TONGUE

"The tongue can bring death or life; those who love to talk will reap the consequences." Proverbs 18:21.

This is where most women and even some men have a huge issue. They just talk too much. The Bible warns us so much about excessive talking. The Bible says to just listen and don't be too quick to even talk. But people just talk talk talk talk talk talk talk talk their way out of their own blessings.

Please Chosen, don't talk too much and mess up your blessings. You want to maximize what God has for you and a key ingredient is to not be too quick to talk.

There is a story in the New Testament that illustrates the importance of this. It is the story of a Jewish priest name Zacharias. Zacharias was married to Elizabeth and the Bible says they were both righteous before God, walking in all the commandments and ordinances of the Lord and were blameless. Which means they were a very blessed and highly favored, Chosen couple. They were now old and passed child baring age, and still childless. They had given up on having a baby and their culture looked at them shamefully for not having the blessing of a child to carry on in the name of the family, per their custom. People are always looking for a way to ridicule the righteous children of God. I'm sure they prayed tirelessly for a baby during their younger years, but now that they were past what man calls child baring years, they seem to have given up believing that God would bless them with a child.

Zacharias went into the temple to burn incense and pray on this particular morning. It was the custom of the Jewish people to have the priest go into the temple and burn the incense twice a day and when the people saw the smoke from the incense they would kneel and pray. The smoke going up towards the heavens symbolized their prayers going up to God.

While Zacharias was in the temple praying, the messenger angel of God named Gabriel in visible and audible form to Zacharias to bring him a message from God. When Zacharias saw Gabriel, he was scared poopless! Remember I told you the angels of God have such a character about them that they always scare people when they reveal themselves in their true form? This very thing happened to Zacharias. The angel had to tell him not to fear and that he was sent with a message from God. I'm sure Zacharias was still scared of the presence and majestic nature of the angel, but he listened to the message non the less.

Gabriel, the angel, told him that his prayer for a son would be answered, and his wife Elizabeth would become pregnant, and he is to name the baby John. Zacharias and Elizabeth are the parents of John the Baptist!

John had to come before his cousin Jesus to make way for the coming messiah and to Baptize Jesus. Gabriel went on to tell Zacharias that he would have joy and gladness, and many would rejoice at the birth of his son. For he will be great om the sight of the Lord and shall not drink any wine or strong drink. He will also be filled with the Holy Spirit, even from his mother's womb! He will turn many of the children of Israel to the Lord their God. He will also go before Him in the spirit and power of Elijah, to change the hearts of people to make ready for the coming of the Lord. He was speaking of Jesus.

Have you ever met someone who feels they were born saved? Born with the Holy Spirit as a young child? That's how John was. The Bible says there is nothing new under the sun and this very thing still happens. There are children still being born today with the Holy Spirit and a Divine Purpose from

God for their lives.

I had "no come to Jesus" moment. I always knew who God was and always had a relationship with the Lord even as a very young child. I was not perfect, and I am human, and I did and still do humanly things which includes things that may be the opposite of what God wants me to do. No human being is without sin. Because you have a relationship with Christ and/or a leadership position amongst the people of God, does not make you perfect or sinless.

For many years Zacharias and Elizabeth prayed for a son. They prayed until they were old enough to figure God just wasn't going to answer that prayer because they were too old to have a baby scientifically or medically according to man. But God! This is a clear case of God does and will answer prayer, but he does so in His time, not ours. Our time is not like God's time. God's timing is right on time! John the Baptist had to come from parents who were blameless and righteous, because John was to be filled with the Holy Spirit in the womb, and he had to be born 6 months before Jesus was born to prepare the way for the Messiah.

After Gabriel shared the wonderful news of their prayers being answered and how great their baby boy would be, Zacharias spoke doubt and disbelief from his lips. This righteous man of faith doubted that God could do such a thing at this old age of his life, and he spoke that from his mouth saying something like this, "Do you really expect me to believe this? I am an old man, and my wife is well advanced in years."

Gabriel with his terrifying self said to Zacharias, "I am Gabriel. (PERIOD) *I stand in the presence of God*, and I have been sent to speak to you and to tell you this good news. And now you will be silent and not able to speak until the day this happens, because you did not believe my words, which will come true at their appointed time."

And Zacharias could no longer talk or speak. He was mute and speechless. This is the power that the angel of the Lord had, he didn't go ask God what he should do with Zacharias in his disbelief, Gabriel called the shots and did what needed to be done. He told Zacharias that what he told him was going to happen was going to come true and to make sure it did, he would prevent Zacharias from further speaking any doubtful words from his mouth. He couldn't even tell Elizabeth about the baby coming and when she realized she was pregnant she hid herself for 5 months. But she was happy because God had answered her prayer, and it would shut the people up who ridiculed her for being barren and without a child.

Zacharias was about to kill his blessing he had been praying for by speaking out loud the disbelief. Gabriel was not having that and doing his duty as a guardian angel and messenger of God, he shut Zacharias up so he wouldn't stop the coming of John the Baptist with his doubtful speaking.

Your words manifest. What you speak and say manifests. You can stop your own blessings by speaking doubt.

Six months later, the angel Gabriel appeared to Mary and told her she would become pregnant with the Son of God. He also told her that her cousin Elizabeth, who they called barren, was six months pregnant. and he ended his conversations with her by saying, "For with God nothing will be impossible."

Mary had faith and believed saying, "Behold the maidservant of the Lord! Let it be to me according to your word." And Gabriel left. He didn't have to make Mary mute and without a voice because she believed. Mary did not speak doubt or negatively. She believed in the miracle and spoke outwardly in belief.

On the eighth day of John's birth, he was to be circumcised and be named after his father. But Elizabeth said no, the baby would be called John. The people didn't like that answer, so they went to Zacharias and asked what to name the baby, and he wrote on a tablet, "His name is John". Immediately Zacharias mouth was opened, and his tongue was loosed, and he spoke, praising God.

It is important, Chosen, that you do not speak against what you are praying for, instead always speak in favor of it. Expect to receive what you are praying for and believe that it is coming in faith. If you don't believe it, don't speak your disbelief out loud. You will still kill your blessing and what you have been praying for if you outwardly speak doubt. Continue to pray for it until your unbelief has turned into belief.

You cannot let the left hand know what the right is doing. Jesus says this in Mathew 6:3, referring to when you give and help others. It's saying not to boast and brag about what you have done for people or the church. Be pure in your heart when you give and silent about your giving.

On another note, you cannot tell people your plans, or anything that you are doing in your personal life. The very people that you think are your friends and family, are the very people that may be speaking outwardly against what you are trying to achieve. Words manifest. Even the words spoken by others on what you are trying to accomplish. If you don't tell them, they can't speak negatively about it.

You don't have a testimony until it has been done and it is over with. If it's still going on it is not a testimony, it is a current situation. Keep it to yourself if you want it to succeed.

Everybody that you think is your friend may not be. People harbor jealousy. Your success weighs heavily on people praying for or against you. Know your circle and choose them wisely. People do change on you, so you must take periodic inventories.

If you aren't sure of certain people, pray to God for answers concerning them. He will let you know who you can trust and who you can't. Psalm 32:8 says, "I will instruct you and teach you in the way you should go; I will counsel you with my eye upon you." God got you, and He will direct your path.

Remember that silence is golden. Just try to be silent more often. I am working hard on this area. Often times I feel as though it's okay to speak exactly what's on my mind to people. Especially when it's a spouse, a close relationship, or with a relative. Sometimes I just say whatever I'm thinking or feeling to them, and I am not aware of how what I am saying is being received or interpreted. This is an area I am admittedly still working on. I need to keep silent most times and keep my thoughts to myself or at least think about how to gently say what my thoughts are.

Another reason to keep silent is because most times people don't really care how we feel or what we think. Nothing bothers me more than that person who could care less about what I am saying or when I am expressing how I feel. I have had the habit of trying to still explain to them when they don't care. If they are not hearing you, just don't waste your time and breath trying to get them to hear you. Forget them and move on to something else. Just stop talking and stop texting. That's what I tell myself. It's a work in progress in this area for me. Texting is still a form of speaking. Because I am a writer, I will text a whole sermon, especially when I'm upset. It is not me being silent at all. Silence is golden for sure. Real G's move in silence.

47

CHAPTER 47

LOVE YOURSELF

Most of us do not love ourselves the way we should. You are your biggest everything. Therefore, make being everything that you are to yourself positive when you fill in the blank. Don't be your biggest discouragement, talking yourself out of chasing your dreams. Be your biggest encouragement and chase your dreams knowing you will achieve them.

Don't be your biggest name caller. Calling yourself dumb, ugly, idiot, stupid. Be your biggest complementor and call yourself smart, beautiful, or handsome, intelligent, magnificent. Magnificent is my personal favorite.

What you think and feel about yourself comes off in an energy that others pick up on and they treat you the way you treat yourself. If you are confident and walking in your good energy, people will respect you and welcome your presence. You can't walk in it unless you feel it. You can lie to yourself, but you can't lie when it comes to the energy you put out into the atmosphere.

You should always look your best. Don't just go anywhere looking like you don't care. If it is a phase or fashion statement that looks that way, don't be a follower. Look your best and don't be in public with a bonnet or a do rag on your head. A cute hat is cool but leave those bonnets and do rags in the bathroom drawer somewhere. Don't wear pajamas out in public unless it's for a holiday or pajama party. Put on a nice outfit and step out like a million dollars every time you walk out the door.

Take pictures of yourself looking fine. Take the pictures for yourself to look at and smile at. They will help make you feel good about yourself and encourage you to continue to look good when you step out of the house. Always snap pictures of yourself with your cellphone. Do what you have to do to build your self-esteem up and keep it up. This will help you achieve your goals because people will want you around.

Always give God your best. Don't give a care about what others may think of how you worship your Heavenly Father. That's a personal relationship and you need to give God your very best. Your mission is for Christ so focus on that.

I am convinced no one has 0 talents. God gives us all at least 1 talent. But many people bury that talent and do nothing with it. They become lazy and wicked with the talents God has given them. No one has an excuse for not using at least their 1 talent. The Bible clearly tells us, "I can do all things through Christ who strengthens me".

The rest is up to you.

Also by Vikki L. Pendleton

Other books by Vikki L. Pendleton:
   KNOWLEDGE NUGGETS
   BECOMING A WEALTHY BELIEVER

Books coming soon:
   BECOMING A WEALTHY BELIEVER PT.3
   AFFIRMATIONS AND EXPLANATIONS

Music, Music Videos, and Social Media for Subscribers and Fans:
   WWW.YOUTUBE.COM/@DJJCHILL
   IG: @dj_jchill

For Bookings:
   contactjchill@gmail.com
   vikki@VikkiLPendleton.com

All related websites:
   FeelizePublishingHouse.com
   FeelizeEntertainment.com
   VikkiLPendleton.com

www.ingramcontent.com/pod-product-compliance
Lightning Source LLC
Chambersburg PA
CBHW060513130626
46553CB00002B/479